I0482815

CEO Tools

(Successful Executive Handbook)

By Ade Asefeso MCIPS MBA

Second Edition

ISBN-13: 978-1499381559
ISBN-10: 1499381557

Publisher: AA Global Sourcing Ltd
Website: http://www.aaglobalsourcing.com

Table of Contents

Disclaimer

This publication is designed to provide competent and reliable information regarding the subject matter covered. However, it is sold with the understanding that the author and publisher are not engaged in rendering professional advice. The authors and publishers specifically disclaim any liability that is incurred from the use or application of contents of this book.

Dedication

To my family and friends who seems to have been sent here to teach me something about who I am supposed to be. They have nurtured me, challenged me, and even opposed me.... But at every juncture has taught me!

This book is dedicated to my lovely boys, Thomas, Michael and Karl. Teaching them to manage their finance will give them the lives they deserve. They have taught me more about life, presence, and energy management than anything I have done in my life.

Part 1: Start-up CEO

Chapter 1: Introduction

Chief Executive Officer (CEO) is the highest ranking executive in a company, whose main responsibilities include developing and implementing high-level strategies, making major corporate decisions, managing the overall operations and resources of a company, and acting as the main point of communication between the board of directors and the corporate operations. The CEO will often have a position on the board, and in some cases is even the chair.

There are various other titles for the position of CEO including president and executive or managing director (MD). The role of the CEO will vary from one company to another depending on its size and organization. In smaller companies, the CEO will often have a much more hands-on role in the company, making a lot of the business decisions; even lower-level ones such as the hiring of staff. However, in larger companies, the CEO will often deal with only the higher-level strategy of the company and directing its overall growth, with most other tasks delegated to managers and departments.

Responsibilities

The responsibilities of an organization's CEO or MD are set by the organization's board of directors or other authority, depending on the organization's legal structure. They can be far-reaching or quite limited and are typically enshrined in a formal delegation of authority.

Typically, the CEO/MD has responsibilities as a director, decision maker, leader, manager and executor. The communicator role can involve the press and the rest of the outside world, as well as the organization's management and employees; the decision-making role involves high-level decisions about policy and strategy. As a leader of the company, the CEO/MD advises the board of directors, motivates employees, and drives change within the organization. As a manager, the CEO/MD presides over the organization's day-to-day operations.

Characteristics

According to a study by Carola Frydman of MIT, from 1936 to the early 2000s there has been a rapid increase in the share of MBA graduates acting as CEOs; from approximately 10% of CEOs in 1960 to more than 50% by the end of the century. Earlier in the century, top executives were more likely to have obtained technical degrees in science and engineering or law degrees.

In some European Union countries, there are two separate boards, one executive board for the day-to-day business and one supervisory board for control purposes (selected by the shareholders). In the US and UK, the CEO presides over the executive board and the chairman presides over the supervisory board, and these two roles will always be held by different people. This ensures a distinction between management by the executive board and governance by the supervisory board. This allows for clear lines of authority. The aim is to prevent a conflict of interest and too much power being concentrated in the hands of one person.

In the United States and United Kingdom, the board of directors (elected by the shareholders) is often equivalent to the supervisory board, while the executive board may often be known as the executive committee (the division/subsidiary heads and C-level officers that report directly to the CEO).

Chapter 2: Start-ups CEO Selection Process

Veterans of the early-stage venture game know that successfully creating a portfolio of promising early-stage companies requires more than hitting the occasional home run. Superior returns harvest the full potential of each promising venture and minimize the odds of each possible failure.

The key to developing this core strength, according to leading investors and company builders, rests on one critical early decision: recruiting the right CEO for the immediate and imminent needs of the venture. No other decision carries the weight of this human capital investment. More than technology and capital, the quality and fit of CEO disproportionately increase the odds that a company will not merely survive, but thrive.

Start-ups have different CEO needs at different points in time. We have identified three distinct phases through which each early-stage CEO must lead a company, from an early round of funding to achieving profitability:
1. Building an effective business model.
2. Bootstrapping the business.
3. Scaling the organization.

1.   Building an Effective Business Model

In this initial stage, the most successful CEOs bring an intense strategic focus to obtain rapid market validation of their business model. They create a clear and concise vision for the company that features a fundable and actionable business plan, all of which creates an acute sense of urgency. Typically, they identify an unmet niche market opportunity and relentlessly pursue it. Sometimes they take a broken business model and reposition or fix it. This is a dynamic and iterative process that continues throughout the life of the company.

2. Bootstrapping the Business

Here is the exceptional quality of execution characterizes superior start-up CEOs. In this phase, the best CEOs demonstrate their operational know-how and ability to prioritize and "right-size." They are productive with limited resources, effectively allocating people and capital to the most promising projects. At the same time, they demonstrate a keen ability to leverage the human capital of employees, customers and investors by spreading the vision of what the company can realize. Their key objective is to validate the business and achieve positive cash flow and market recognition rapidly.

3. Scaling the Organization

This phase demands the ability to direct and delegate in order to build a robust and well-rounded infrastructure for growth. CEO prioritizes the responsibility of recruiting, training and supporting the best talent. This team building emphasis is important at all phases of the business, but it is especially critical when CEO needs to step back from managing all aspects of the business. His or her objective is to recruit an "A" team that can collectively out-think and out-execute the competition over time. CEO makes sure that everyone focuses on revenue growth that leads to market dominance.

The Impact of an Early Stage CEO

CEO is almost always the key driver in each of these three phases of an early-stage company. He or she, with the support of the Board of Directors, is the only agent with the necessary breadth and business perspective to make the most important decisions in each of these three phases. Yet finding the right fit requires more than checking off a simple list of desired qualities.

Selecting the right CEO is essentially about prioritizing the needs for the business, matching the identified competencies with CEO's core set of skills, and ranking the short list of CEO's skill set, which will enable him/her to execute the business plan successfully. Moreover, it requires a keen understanding of a company's life cycle and an appreciation for the specific challenges required to lead it through its next stages of growth.

The management competencies closely correlate to the three phases in the Early Stage Value Creation Cycle discussed earlier. Our experience suggests that venture firms, boards and management teams would be much better off structuring the search process, evaluation criteria and assessment methodology around these few key business requirements and CEO competencies, which consistently emerge as the hallmarks that separate winning CEOs and companies from the losers.

Our suggestions are just as powerfully effective for avoiding mistakes as they are for insuring success. Just as the right CEO can often create the right conditions for a promising start-up to thrive, the wrong CEO can, and often does, sink an early-stage company. Many CEO candidates look attractive

13

on paper, with great contacts and a record of apparent success in relevant high-growth technology organizations, but such credits can falsely sell someone who was simply in the right place at the right time or enjoyed other non-replicable conditions. Many technology executives have been momentum players and simply do not have the core competencies or raw energy to successfully build an early-stage technology company in today's difficult and volatile environment.

Let's now examine each of the phases in more depth:

Phase 1: Building an Effective Business Model

Competency one: Dynamic Business Acumen

CEO Must Do's
- Crystallize the Idea
- Evolve the Model
- Evangelize

Interestingly, we found over and over that the highest ranked CEOs are not necessarily those associated with the best companies. CEOs who received the highest marks have often taken broken businesses and business plans and worked with the management team, board, customers and other stakeholders to develop a viable business model and create competitive positioning that earns the confidence of the market and investors. Some of these CEOs are founders who have grown and evolved their companies over time. Others are professional managers who were brought in to re-start a company or take it into new markets.

Above all, the most important trait for this phase is the ability to develop and articulate a very clear value proposition and investment thesis for a company as an iterative process.

These individuals are strategic builders who understand how their company fits into the overall competitive ecosystem and who can create a "must have" product that delivers specific value to customers, partners and potential acquirers. They are great evangelists and nearly obsessive communicators with all stakeholders at all times. They demonstrate the ability to persuade investors to invest in the company, potential clients to test their product and proven executives to join the firm. One example can be seen in an e-commerce business that was recently sold for a substantial amount to a larger organization. In this case, the founder/CEO came up with an idea for a new way to provide information to customers in an important vertical market segment, but the initial revenue models were not compelling to the company or its venture backers. CEO then led the organization through an intensive period of analysis, business modelling and trial and error before finding an innovative way to drive significant revenues for its business partners at relatively little cost to the company. The organization was able to extract a meaningful cut of each transaction and drive tremendous growth and profitability with relatively few people in the organization, eventually leading to a lucrative strategic sale for its management team and shareholders.

On the other hand, CEOs who were not highly ranked in this category were unable to respond to difficult market conditions. The venture capitalists we surveyed were frustrated by those CEOs, who are not able to develop a viable value proposition or investment thesis, and often withdrew their support from the company. Faced with a failing business model, these CEOs failed to adapt it to a successful one.

Phase 2: Bootstrapping the Business

Competency Two: Operational Vigilance and Efficiency
CEO Must Do's
- Allocate Resources Efficiently
- Evolve the Model
- Evangelize

In the second phase of a start-up's growth, CEOs must display a more hands-on, operational expertise. In addition to having outstanding strategic skills, a strong customer orientation/focus and business model acumen, the best CEOs are also highly disciplined operating executives who can "right-size" an organization at this crucial moment. This means establishing a platform for growth by optimizing cash and resources while building the company block by block. These individuals prioritize every product decision and customer engagement to create saleable building blocks for the future, rather than distracting the company with conflicting short-term opportunities.

This is not as simple as cutting costs and managing tight budgets. The most successful CEOs align the company's resources and cash with the right short list of priorities to execute its strategic vision. If the model is broken and the company needs six months to reposition itself, the right CEOs have the foresight to make drastic cuts in the organization to conserve cash and allow time for the company to recover. If there is a large, time-sensitive market opportunity, the right CEOs are able to identify and justify the investments required to capitalize on that opportunity.

16

They also understand the nature of the competitive game and bring a sense of urgency to the execution of the business plan.

It is important to note that there are few CEOs who combine both a strategic orientation and such a high level of operating discipline. Yet the ability to align a company's strategic vision and real-time operating plan is critical to an early-stage company's success in a resource-constrained environment. Successful early-stage CEOs run very lean, flat organizations and are very close to the markets that they serve. These individuals are directly involved with customers and nimbly direct resources toward specific market opportunities, aligning the interests of the product development team, services organization and related functions. They spend where and when it really matters.

Several venture firms relayed their experience with a software organization that had raised a significant amount of venture financing, but had not yet reached profitability. The existing CEO had overbuilt the company relative to the current prospects for the business and had not been able to expand it beyond its initial market niche. In this situation, the company embarked on a search for a new CEO, eventually recruiting an individual who was known to the organization. He was able to quickly right-size the company based on the immediate market opportunity while driving a thoughtful review of new market opportunities and delivery models. The company was soon able to achieve breakeven profitability while directing limited resources to a series of targeted new business opportunities, which now represent growth prospects for the company. Moreover, without the addition of significant new resources, this organization was able to reinstill a sense of urgency and focus, which enabled a dramatic improvement in productivity. Throughout this period, the new CEO actively communicated with the management team and board of directors, thereby insuring buy-in to both short-term changes and longer-term strategic direction.

The "evil twins" for the executives who effectively bootstrapped their businesses were demonstrated by CEOs who often had unreasonably optimistic expectations for the business and failed to allocate resources or right-size operations efficiently, often running out of cash before the business had a chance to succeed.

Phase 3: Scaling the Business

Competency Three: Team Builder Quotient

CEO Must Do's
- Upgrade the Team
- Develop Infrastructure
- Expand the Business

As a start-up enters this third phase of growth, the best CEOs emerge as market leaders and great team builders. They understand that revenue growth is important to building market momentum and eventually reaching market leadership. From a business perspective, it is important for CEO to establish market dominance in one specific market that can be used as a beachhead for further expansion into new products and/or new markets. This is critical to stabilizing the company business model and becoming cash flow positive. At the same time, they take full responsibility for establishing and retaining a winning team, as well as building long-term, sustainable barriers to competition.

They recognize their own strengths and weaknesses and are able to attract and retain the best executives with the right portfolio of experience and skills to complement their own. This is a critical point. Many companies and boards make the mistake of trying to find all the skills needed for the company in one individual, CEO. Clearly, no single individual can check every box in terms of operating skills, functional experience, domain knowledge, etc. The most successful CEOs of winning portfolio companies have a knowledge for recruiting a strong operating team with a complementary mix of experience in sales, marketing, product development, support, finance, HR, and operations. Indeed, one intriguing finding is that CEO excellence at this level transcends industry expertise or top-rate networks. Respondents said the best CEOs do not necessarily have to have a directly relevant domain of experience and the perfect Rolodex. The top quartile of our survey reported that the best CEOs were often talented leaders who, from the very beginning, focused on creating a winning environment and recruiting individuals who represented a culture fit with their existing team.

One venture firm cited a recent case of a high-growth venture that recruited an experienced chief executive officer to complement a group of founding partners. The organization had an extremely strong corporate culture and business model, but was struggling to keep up with the demands of the business as it scaled exponentially. In this situation, CEO brought very complementary operational and sales and marketing skills to an organization that had been built around its technical founders. The ability of this new CEO to successfully leverage the assets that had made the company successful, while focusing on additional hiring and initiatives in those areas most critical to supporting its growth, was instrumental in his success in positioning the business for a successful exit. In addition, CEO played a critical role in helping broaden the footprint of the business in a way that accelerated its growth trajectory while creating additional barriers to entry.

Statements used by the venture partners to describe successful CEOs with the ability to scale the business and retain "A" teams are:

- "Everyone wants to work for the team."
- "They had an eye for talent and a strong ability to attract some of the best in the business."
- "For them, it is all about winning the Super Bowl not just the game."
- "They were relentless in their pursuit of their objectives and they never gave up."
- "They were inspirational and passionate about their business."

On the other hand, the worst CEOs in this category were characterized as failures as leaders, often having large egos, lacking urgency, failing to listen, being overly protective, hiring weak teams and not firing "C players." Even, worse, these CEOs were reported to have a tendency to often withdraw protectively and withhold data at the very times when they should have been actively soliciting help from the team and from the board, thereby compounding problems even further.

Improving the Odds

A friend of mine once said, "I invest in people, not ideas." He clearly understood the value of assessing a potential CEO on many dimensions, not just financial success of former ventures. In our experience, we have found that most venture capital firms would benefit by having a set process or objective assessment framework for evaluating talent beyond standard resumes, interviews and referencing that are surprisingly cursory in nature.

This chapter provide a practical, predictive tool to determine whether a candidate (or incumbent CEO) you are considering is likely to add a winner to your portfolio or increase the risk of the new venture failing. This is particularly important, since the pool of existing, previously successful start-up CEOs is extremely limited. The fact is that a large percentage of early-stage executives work hard to get their first "win" and then often move on to other activities such as board work, venture partner roles, etc. There is no training "academy," like General Electric, that generates a meaningful pool of proven, trained start-up CEOs. We hope this chapter will help start-up organizations and their boards separate winning and losing CEO candidates through the use of four key diagnostic elements: competency based interviews, referencing, benchmarking and psychometric tests.

Competency Based Interviews

The most important step in the evaluation of a prospective CEO is the ability to link a candidate's prior successes and failures to the particular attributes required to perform in a specific job. These competency based interviews are more effective than standard interviews in two ways. They involve a focus on the distinctive CEO competencies related to success (such as those outlined in Phases 1, 2 and 3 above), and they involve the collection of tangible evidence about a candidate's level of effectiveness in previous jobs, thereby providing precision, practicality and relevance to the insights derived from the interview.

Even the most experienced venture capitalist often falls into the interview trap of focusing on the story of the resume rather than the specific CEO competencies required to build an early-stage business. But in a competency-based interview, an artful candidate cannot wax on about how he would address a hypothetical situation involving, for example, cash constraints. These techniques help to tell the difference between "I would' and "I did" very significant to predicting future actions, particularly when in a stressful situation where the stakes are big.

Referencing

Next comes validation from the most trusted source, knowledgeable references. The epitome of good leadership centres on the effective and substantial impact of an individual on a given constituency. Virtually all CEO candidates have a history. The real question is whether the candidate's characterization of his or her impact matches their previous team's description. Will future teams follow this leader? Or is he/she a legend in their own mind? Did a previous board support this individual or was he/she pushed out?

When conducted well, reference conversations with a CEO candidate's previous team can yield useful insights about that candidate's level of effectiveness.

Benchmarking

For an early-stage company to become a forerunner in its field, it is not enough to simply have an acceptable or passable CEO. The objective should be to have the "best" CEO among all those organizations with which a company competes in the marketplace. A handful of the top recruiting firms interview CEO candidates for early-stage companies on a frequent basis. No other professional is as well suited to understand how a candidate fits into a specific talent market. A search committee or Board of an early-stage company may not have as broad a view of the spectrum of talent in a certain industry segment or they may want a second opinion given the gravity of the decision involved. We believe the search committee or Board should, at a minimum, identify CEOs in the top five to 10 competitors, and then compare and contrast their capabilities to specific CEO candidates.

Psychometric Testing

More than ever, there is a realization that thinking, communication and relationship styles have as strong a correlation to CEO performance in general, as they do to the three early-stage competencies. For example, business acumen involves a rare combination of critical and adaptive thinking, creativity and detail orientation. Bootstrapping requires watchfulness, flexibility, prioritization, assertiveness and boundary setting. Scaling and team building to create market leadership necessitates insight into others, motivation and drive, persuasiveness, and relationship building skills. These "under the skin" traits in candidates can be measured via several well-developed and well-chosen questionnaires. There are five types of questionnaires often used by professional and qualified assessors, which measure: leadership and work style, level of motivation and preferred work environments, derailers or factors that may cause a previously successful manager to fail, match to organizational culture, and if important for the situation and desired by the client thinking and critical reasoning.

We should note that these early-stage CEO assessment tools are not only useful for evaluating prospective CEO candidates. They are also important for evaluating and monitoring existing talent and, if used properly, may reveal CEO performance issues well before they are reflected in standard business or financial metrics and when it may be too late. A diligent early-stage board is well served by having an ongoing review of its CEO (as well as other key leaders) along each of these dimensions.

Chapter 3: How to Be Start-up CEO

Being CEO of a start-up is one of the most challenging roles out there. Your job is to build a product customers love; recruit a team; find funding from customers, partners, or investors; and guide the overall prioritization of work.

In my experience the three most important components of the Start-up CEO's role are:

- Creating a product that solves a real customer need (and convincing customers to pay for it).
- Making sure your users and customers have an extremely positive emotional experience with your product.
- Recruiting a great team to build your product.

Yes, you are also in charge of incorporating, finding a place to work, creating the foundations of your culture, hiring your first employees, setting up a bank account, creating a web site, finding early stage funding, and taking out the trash. You are basically the Chief Everything Officer at this early stage.

But these activities matter little if you can't figure out how to create something of value and convince others to pay for it in an exchange that benefits both parties. Figuring out your value proposition in other words, what you sell that brings value to others is key in this early stage. Once you show there is market demand for your core value proposition (in other words, "have happy paying customers"), the remaining steps in building a business are relatively easy.

Here is what I learned at AA Global Sourcing about being a start-up CEO.

When you first start your business you will need to determine who gets what percentage of the company. The initial levels of ownership are determined when you file your incorporation paperwork. If there is no one else involved then you will simply own all the outstanding shares and 100% of the corporation. If there are other individuals involved then you will need to negotiate what is a fair percentage for them to receive and for you to receive.

There are some key factors to take into consideration when deciding who should get what at the formation of a company.

These factors include:
- What role in the organization will each person have once the business is incorporated?
- How much time will each person be putting in going forward?
- How much money is each person putting in at the start of the company?
- How much business and entrepreneurship experience does each person have?
- Will one party be contributing any existing intellectual property to the new corporation?

If there are multiple parties involved, it is important to vest ownership over a period of years to make sure they don't walk away with the full amount if they quit after six months. The most common vesting timeframe is four years with a one year cliff, which means that they get nothing if they leave in the first 364 days, 25% from day 365-730, 50% from day 730-1095, and so on. Personally, I find it is better for employees and the company to do a shorter cliff (3 months) and extend vesting to 6 years so that you can give a bit more equity up front at the lower current fair market value rather than wait 4 years and have to make a second grant at a higher price.

If you are partnering with an experienced entrepreneur or engineer who has had multiple successes and lots of contacts and who will be putting in hundreds of thousands of dollars of their own money and working full-time on the venture together with you, expect to have to give up a lot more than if you are partnering with a first time entrepreneur or engineer with little business experience who will only be working on the venture 20 hours per week.

I recommend not splitting a company 50:50, as it will cause deadlocks. It is generally a good thing for the speed of decision-making for one person to have more than 50% of the shares (and thus the vote). Figuring out which person this should be is up to negotiation. If needed, you can ask your lawyer to divvy up the shareholder vote differently than the economic interests by creating separate class of stock with extra voting rights.

Incorporating

There are many important reasons to incorporate your business. The most important benefits of incorporation are:
- You are taken more seriously by prospects, vendors, potential employees, and potential investors.
- You are able to open a business bank account and begin to build credit for your business.
- You are able to protect yourself from some personal liability.
- You pay less taxes. As an individual, you effectively pay taxes on your total income (with a few allowed

deductions). As a business, you pay taxes on your net income.

You can either incorporate via a local law firm (for around $2000) or incorporate online using a service like incorporate.com or legalzoom.com for about $350 in the US. In the UK you can incorporate via Company House online using a web service at www.companieshouse.gov.uk

The most common state and entity type for companies who want to raise outside investment is a Delaware C Corporation, due to the business friendly/investor friendly standardized case law in Delaware. If you incorporate in a State other than the one in which your business operates, you will need to pay another $150 or so per year for what's called a Registered Agent. I'd recommend consulting an attorney to decide whether to form an LLC, S Corp, or C Corp and to determine in which State it is best for you to incorporate your business.

Keeping Costs Extremely Low

You may be in need of funding prior to being able to develop your product or service. My strong recommendation is to raise as little money as possible but enough to get the first iteration of your product or service to market. Be as creative as you can, offering ownership in your company in exchange for early employees' work or for critical services like legal and accounting, or requesting deferred payment so that you can pay when you are able to. Keep your costs down, as low as possible, until your monthly revenues grow and enable you to increase your expenses. And do contract consulting work on the side if needed to have money to live on.

If there is a key skill-set you need to be able to produce and sell your product that you don't have (say, programming or sales), instead of looking for an employee who you have to pay, look for a business partner who will take equity in the company, vesting over time, and who will be willing to take only a very minimal salary and defer it for a couple years.

If you are working on creating a software product, you can also use sites like elance.com, odesk.com, guru.com, or smarterwork.com to find contractors willing to develop your software at a low cost.

When my partner and I started working on AA Global Sourcing in 2010, we deferred our salaries for one year. We survived by keeping company and personal costs extremely low and by doing consulting work on the side. I kept my monthly personal expenses under £1000 by living in the office that first summer and eating lots of Ramen Noodles. We didn't have any other choice.

If you are an experienced entrepreneur and have sold a company for more than $25 million in the past, raising funding for your new venture won't be difficult. But beware that sometimes having funding is more of a curse than a benefit because it removes the pressure to get customers to pay for your product, which is generally a good pressure to have. If you are a first time entrepreneur, raising outside funding will be very difficult until you can prove that you can sell something to somebody. Debt funding won't be available either until your business is turning a monthly profit, unless you have personal or corporate assets you can secure the loan against.

Understanding the Role of the Entrepreneur

Growing up in UK, I didn't really know much about entrepreneurship and business, but as I began working in companies around the age of 21 and 22, and started my company, AA global Sourcing, I discovered that there is an entirely different world out there. In fact, there is a world of prosperity and great wealth out there for you to reach for. You can enter this world. But first, you have to be aware that it exists and you have to work hard to create value for others.

There are multiple ways to build wealth over time through entrepreneurship. You can take an annual salary, you can take profit distributions (dividends), and you can sell stock in the company that you own (later on, when it has revenues and profits) either in private markets through firms like Second Market or in public markets via an IPO. A successful entrepreneur who builds a strong team and brings immense value to a large customer base can earn tens or sometimes hundreds of millions of dollars for changing an industry.

It is the entrepreneur's role to bring together the people and resources necessary to build your product and company. An entrepreneur takes initiative and has a bias toward action, has the ability to take feedback, has a high tolerance for stress and is very determined. An entrepreneur also has decisiveness, courage, and the ability to deal with failure. An entrepreneur is often someone who is quite creative, has the ability to learn quickly, and perseveres through nearly anything. An entrepreneur can delay gratification and has a drive to achieve and the abilities to plan, build a team, inspire and lead, and prioritize.

The "I Just Need $250,000 to Get Started" Complaint

When I hear first-time entrepreneurs say, "All I need is $250,000 to start my business and as soon as I raise this money I will be able to get started," I get concerned for them. Unless they have a wealthy family member who is willing to take a big bet, I worry they are going to spend the next nine months of their lives trying to raise this money, only to find it is not available or not available at terms they can live with.

Instead of planning to raise $250,000 and then getting started, plan to raise $10,000 from your own savings and close friends and:

Incorporate.
- Figure out how to convince people to work for you for next to nothing (in exchange for equity and deferred salary).
- Create a product or service that you can sell.
- Start selling.
- Use the revenue you are making to finance future product improvements and development.
- Once you get to $15,000 per month in sales, then go look for seed funding to improve your product scale up your model if needed!

Filtering Out the "Talkers" from the "Doers"

It may take you a year or more to get your business to $15,000 per month in sales. That is okay. Generating revenue for your business without much outside capital is really hard. It is supposed to be. There are millions of people with great business ideas, but only a select few, perhaps 2-3%, can take their idea and execute by turning them into something that people will pay for, over and over.

This difficult process filters out talkers from doers. Most people are talkers. Investors know that investing in someone who has figured out how to create something from nothing (creating a solution to a need that people will pay to have solved) provides a much higher chance of generating a return than investing in someone who just has an idea and "needs" your money to even get started. Entrepreneurs who simply "can't" get started on anything until they get lots of funding must learn to become much more resourceful and figure out how to pull together an initial product that customers will pay for or at least a prototype that proves there is demand.

Creating Something from Nothing

The act of "creating something from nothing" cannot be modelled in a Goldman Sachs spreadsheet. It is the magic that entrepreneurs and entrepreneurial engineers have. This is, definitionally, what entrepreneurs do; bring together the resources of land, labour, capital, and entrepreneurial ability to create something of value that is greater than the cost of the sum of inputs and sell it to the marketplace.

Once you get to, say, $15,000 per month in recurring revenue, it will be so much easier to raise equity funding. Don't wait until you are there to start building relationships with investors but do wait until your business has existing revenue before you actually ask for their money. You will receive much better terms and give up a lot less control and ownership. Firms like Instagram that sell for hundreds of millions of dollars without generating revenue are extraordinarily rare and unfortunately have the side effect of inspiring lots of companies to get started and invest time in a product that has no way of generating revenue.

I am not saying that if investment funding is available pre-revenue, don't take it. I am saying that in most cases, as a first time entrepreneur, investment funding pre-revenue will simply not be available without a herculean effort that may end up diluting you so much that you wish you had found a way to fund initial expenses with sales or personal funds.

By focusing on building a real company (with happy paying customers and growing revenue) rather than an app with no clear revenue model, you will have a higher chance of creating a sustainable business in which revenues are greater than expenses. Sustainability of cash flows buys you time and it prevents costly dilution. Time is a good thing to have in business. Cash flow is king, as they say.

Chapter 4: Being a CEO with 1-5 Employees

Once you have employees, you transition from being the Chief Everything Officer to the Chief Energy Officer. It is no longer your job to do everything. Now, you get things done based on the quality of the team around you and your ability to clearly communicate and guide the team toward a shared outcome.

Two really crazy things happen when you hire your first employee. Suddenly you are responsible for the livelihood for another human being. And now you have to manage someone.

If you have been a parent, you have nothing to worry about. Managing an employee is much easier than managing a child. But if you have never been a parent before, watch out. Your life forever changes as a CEO when it's no longer just you and a partner or two to worry about. The most important things to know about management are this:

- Only hire people who can do their job better than you could.
- Hire people who have a positive attitude, have a strong work-ethic, and can communicate effectively.
- Hire people who are motivated intrinsically by the mission the company is focused on achieving (make sure you define what change your company is focused on making in the world extremely clearly on your web site, in recruiting, and to all candidates. The best candidates are driven by purpose and impact, not money).
- Communicate clearly where the team is going.

- Set up an objective system in advance to track performance to pre-set communicated goals.
- Trust people to do their job. Don't micromanage.
- Let go of people quickly if they aren't performing and hitting their goals. Never keep underperformers around for more than 30 days as they will drag the whole team down and lower the bar for the existing team as well as all future hires.

Your first few hires will absolutely be critical in the long term success of your business. But know that you won't get it perfectly right no matter what you do. The most important thing is that you hire someone to begin taking over the basic operational tasks. If they are not right, you can get someone else. You must begin the process of scaling yourself by hiring others who can free up your time to focus on growing the business instead of working in the business. If you don't, you will forever have a job and never a business.

The Importance of Making the First Hire

I will tell a quick story illustrating the importance of making the first hire. I built a web site for a lady named Andrea. Andrea was a flight attendant with a major Airline. She would fly on the international routes to China once a month. She began bringing back freshwater pearl necklaces, pendants, rings, and earrings to sell to her friends. They became quite popular and she would get many requests.

When Andrea and I met in the spring of 2010, she asked if I could build a web site for her. She incorporated and we set up the merchant account, shopping cart, and ecommerce store. We got listed in the major search engines. Six months in, her company was up to about $5000 per month in sales and about $1500 per month in net profit. She came to a critical decision point. Should she continue to do everything herself or hire her first employee to take over customer service and product fulfilment?

Andréa decided that she would give up too much of her profit if she hired someone, so continued to do the customer service and product fulfilment herself. The business continued to grow. By month nine the business was up to about $7,000 per month in sales and $2,000 per month in profit. But after going through some family issues, Andrea decided to shut down the business because the $2000 per month she was making wasn't worth the hassle to her. Andrea no doubt lost out on a multi-million dollar opportunity by choosing to shut the business down rather than taking a leap of faith and hiring her first employee and beginning to scale the organization.

I learned the key lesson that as soon as you can afford to, hire your first employee, even if you have to use every single dollar of net profit you have to do it. Hiring this person will enable you to focus on growing the business well beyond its current level.

Hiring Your First Employees

When I started working at AA Global Sourcing Ltd in the summer of 2010, I would sleep in the office on a futon. I did wake up at 2AM or 3AM, roll out of bed to the desk and just start typing. I did work until 7PM, go have "dinner" at McDonald's, then go to sleep and put the schedule on repeat most nights. Only when Andy, my friend at the time, came over would I adjust the schedule a bit. For those first few months, my business partner and I, with occasional help from a couple of friends of ours, were the only ones working at AA Global Sourcing Ltd.

Once we hired our first employee, suddenly I had to think about having more "normal" working hours. I got an apartment a few miles away and would come in at the very early hour of 7AM; way earlier than my internal clock would have told me.

We hired John as an intern to help us with picking up the phone when customers would call needing help. We had put up a flyer at local business school advertising an internship at "AA Global Sourcing Ltd a Start-up." We named John our "VP of Customer Service." After a month, we agreed to pay him $1000 per month plus 7% of the company (which was a bit too much, but fortunately we vested it over four years) to stay on and do both our customer service and marketing. John stayed for eight months until his fiancée graduated from accounting school and moved to Texas to do a Masters in Advertising. One of John's first responsibilities was to send out a press release to the local news about the company. The Local Paper picked up the story. This article was how we found our second employee, David.

David was a 51-year-old who had significant business experience as an accountant and a truffles salesman. He joined our team as our VP of Business Development and took a salary of just $30,000 per year and negotiated 15% of the company. David brought a lot to the company by way of the respect we gained from having an actual adult and experienced business person on our team. He led our Business Development efforts for 3 years before leaving AA Global Sourcing Ltd in 2013.

Turning Your Job into a Business

It's an exciting time when you are hiring your first employees. You are in the process of turning a job into a true business. If your business isn't making money while you are sleeping, you have a job and not a business. And if you can't take two months off and come back to find your business doing better than when you left, you have a job and not a business. Hiring your first team members is the first step in this process of removing yourself from the day to day operations so you can work on the business instead of in the business.

During this phase, do all you can to enable the company to survive. You should be in charge of product development or sales, or both. Keep your costs low and focus on product development and sales. "Sell, sell, sell" should be your motto, with "listen, listen, listen" as a secondary mantra, representing the need to incorporate customer feedback to make your offering better so you can sell even more.

Chapter 5: Characteristics of a Good Start-up CEO

Now that it's more than just you, it's worth sharing some of the characteristics of a good Chief Executive Officer.

- Ability to understand the needs of the customer
- Ability to create products that solve the customer need
- Confidence
- Humility
- Aptitude for public speaking
- Ability to communicate a vision
- Ability to authentically care about employees and customers
- Desire to work hard

Building an Advisory Board

Surrounding yourself with individuals much more experienced than yourself, who have already achieved what you want to achieve, is critical to your ability to quickly learn what you need to learn in order to succeed in building your business. I strongly recommend spending some time identifying people who have already done what you want to do and reaching out to them. Invite them to coffee and lunch. Probably 2 out of 10 people you reach out to will say yes. You can double this success ratio by getting an introduction from someone you know who also knows them.

Take these potential mentors out to lunch and tell them briefly what you do and then ask them questions. Don't try to sell them on anything or convince them to invest or join anything yet. At the end of the first meeting, tell them you really enjoyed meeting with them and ask if you could meet again in 2-3 months once you have made some further progress. Almost everyone will say yes to this request if made in person, simply because they know that so few people actually follow up in these cases.

Two months later, follow up and schedule a second lunch or coffee. At the end of the second lunch or coffee with your prospective mentor, you will have done what only 5% of the people who have ever asked them for help have ever done. You have met with them twice. At this point, ask if they did be willing to meet with you once per quarter. If you want, you can also ask if you can list them as a member of your informal advisory board on your website or in your investor deck. Now, you have got them, and as long as you curate the relationship carefully over time, they will always be available to you as a mentor and guide.

The mistake most people make in building an advisory board is asking people to join something formal with a defined commitment after one hour of talking. Most busy people don't have time for another formal commitment, except to individuals they have known for years. So build the relationship over time and then ask for an informal commitment. As they get to know you and your business and see you actually doing what you say you are going to do (something 98% of people do not, for some reason!), they will be more and more willing to help you. Why? Because they get the benefit of giving back and perhaps being able to brag to their friends that they were part of something that became successful at the very early stages.

Setting up Office Space

Once you have a few employees, it may be time to find some space for people to work out of. You can probably keep working out of your house or garage until your team numbers around five people, but once you get there it may be time to sign a lease. You can work with a commercial real estate broker for free (the builder owner usually pays their fee) so it is worth reaching out to one to get their assistance in finding the right space for your business. In the early stages, keep your monthly costs as low as possible and your length of commitment as short as possible.

Avoiding Micromanagement

One of the biggest mistakes I made as a young manager was being a micromanager. I would give unclear directions and then come back the next day and suggest minute changes, like adjusting the font size on something. I can only imagine that it was a bit frustrating working for me in those early days.

I learned later that the only way to scale yourself is to hire individuals who can do their job much better than you could do their job and to set goals with them and hold them accountable to their goals but not to tell them how to do their job. My business partner and I learned early that a business can only scale its revenues as fast as the quality of the people it hires.

Setting Up an Accounting System

Make sure you hire a bookkeeper to keep track of and categorize your revenues and expenses (and if you can't afford one, learn how to do it yourself). Have them send you a monthly income statement, balance sheet, and cash flow statement. Learn how to read a financial statement if you don't know how. It's up to you if you want to see you statements in a cash basis or accrual basis.

Most common accounting packages like QuickBooks and Peachtree or (or online accounting tools like Xero, Kashoo, or Legerble) can produce both cash basis and accrual basis reports. You will need an accounting system set up to be able to raise investment later.

Cash is King

At this point in your business's early existence, cash is king. The most important figure is the amount of cash you have in the bank, with the second most important figure being the amount of outstanding checks you have. Your job is to do everything necessary to keep the bank balance above zero.

With two to five employees, you don't need to worry yet about communication or processes, especially if you are all working within a few feet of each other. Just survive and get a product to market that you can sell over and over and constantly improve. Put every dollar you make back into people, product, technology, sales, and marketing.

Holding Your First Board Meeting

There are certain things you have to do in order to make sure your status as a corporation is protected. The most important thing is to make sure you have a separate bank account for your business and to make sure you don't run personal expenses through the business bank account.

The second thing you need to do is to hold a meeting of your Board of Directors at least annually and take and capture minutes from the meeting. In the beginning, you or you and your business partner may be the only Board Member(s). That is okay. You can add other board members later if you raise funding.

Document the attendees and decisions the Board makes in your minutes and file them away. Your law firm can provide forms to help you capture the minutes. Over time, you will build a professional Board of Directors who can serve as mentors and guides as the business grows into new levels of complexity.

Chapter 6: Being a CEO With 6-25 Employees

Congratulations. You have six employees. You are running a real business. You have revenues approaching $25,000 per month (you'd better, or else what are you doing with all those employees?!). If you took a month off, the business would probably still be there when you got back.

Now, it's time to:
- Put in place some basic systems and tools to automate your operations and prepare for growth.
- Figure out your customer unit economics so you can determine whether it makes sense to raise outside capital to scale your customer acquisition.

And as your revenue growth allows:
- Hire a really good person to own marketing.
- Hire a really good person to own customer service.
- Hire a really good person to own sales.
- Hire a really good person to own R&D/product development.
- Hire an in-house bookkeeper or controller to own accounting.
- Hire a really good administrative assistant who enables you to maximize your productivity.

Ask yourself, what is your specialty? What are you good at? Most early-stage CEOs are either really good at sales, marketing, and product vision or really good at technology and R&D. Find someone to own what you are not good at.

You should never have more than seven direct reports. So once you get to eight employees including yourself, you will have to create your first layer of management. Most often this is done by functional area, with all the operations reps reporting to the Director of Operations, the developers reporting to the Technical Director, the sales reps reporting to the Director of Sales, etc. and all the Directors reporting to you.

Instead of starting out by naming every early employee a VP like we did, I would recommend avoiding the VP title for the first couple years of your business. While you are still under 25 employees, just call someone a Director or Manager if you can. Only once you have more than 7 directors will you need a VP title. This title structure will help you reduce the chances of having to later demote early VPs to Director roles as the organization scales.

Creating a Basic Meeting Rhythm

As you move beyond working in a single room, creating a basic meeting structure will be helpful.

When we had 6-25 employees at AA Global Sourcing Ltd we simply had a weekly staff meeting with everyone in the company back when we could actually fit everyone in one room!

Every week, we reviewed the company's weekly results (sales, trials, conversions), tracked progress against each of our quarterly priorities, and reviewed the status of each of our company-wide projects. We eventually came up with Key Performance Indicators and quantitative measures of success and started marking each KPI as red, yellow, green, or super-green based on how we were performing. We were as objective as possible about results, and did our best to leave subjectivity out of the assessments. By making it clear in advance which metrics individuals were responsible for and would be compensated on, we had an easier time assessing performance later.

We would also hold a company-wide offsite every six months called AA Global Day at which we talked about strategy and the future of the business.

At 100 employees, we had a more complex meeting rhythm that consisted of a weekly Senior Leadership Team (SLT) Meeting, a weekly Operating Committee Meeting, monthly company-wide meetings, quarterly company-wide kickoffs, and quarterly SLT offsites on team health, operations, and strategy.

By this stage, our weekly meeting consisted of the six-member Senior Leadership Team (CEO, CTO, CFO, COO, VP Sales, VP HR) and another six members of what we call the Operating Committee. At this weekly meeting we did three things:

1. Quarterly Priorities Review: Have the Operating Committee owner of each quarterly priority report on its progress.
2. KPI Review: Review the Red, Yellow, Green, Super-green coded results for about 8 company-wide metrics plus about sixty departmental metrics, tracked weekly via a Google Doc (we should have fully automated this!).
3. Announcements and Open Agenda Items: Anyone can bring anything up for discussion.

Defining Your Company Values

Back in 2010, we defined our company values. For three years we had a list of ten company values. We printed them up on big cardstock boards and had everyone sign the back at each AA Global Day.
There was only one problem. No one could remember them. I once tried to recall the values without looking at the sheet and got to four before my memory failed me.

We had to re-do our values; make them unique to us and easy to remember.

On a Thursday in December 2009, our Senior Leadership Team met for a two-day offsite to create our first ever One Page Strategic Plan (OPSP) following a format that comes from the book The Rockefeller Habits. The OPSP has a very visible section on the left side within which you are supposed to put your values. We took the entire first day to redefine our company's values.
Our facilitator, started out by asking us to write down the five words that we felt most described our company culture. When we were done, he wrote all the words, perhaps 30 in total, on a flipchart. He found the commonalities amongst similar words and got us down to eight words that defined our culture. He then had us each vote for three.

Patrick took the tally and it was clear what our top values were. There was a tie between five and six and so we debated for about an hour over which one was truly more important and more descriptive. We eventually settled on incorporating number five, "Have Fun and Be Wacky," into the descriptive language underneath another value.

50

Finally, we needed to create an acronym that would make it easy for everyone in the company to remember the values.

We started out with

- "Wow the Customer"
- "Operate With Excellence"
- "Act With Urgency"
- "Treat People With Respect"
- "Act Like an Owner"

We didn't want to have WOATA be our values acronym! After two hours of restructuring we came up with:

- "Wow the Customer"
- "Operate With Urgency"
- "Work Without Mediocrity"
- "Make a Positive Wake"
- "Engage as an Owner"

We got it. Our values acronym was WOWME! Much better. We rolled out WOWME a few weeks later on January 9th, 2013, and immediately integrated our values into everything we did, from our training to employee recognition system to our performance reviews. We made sure chanting WOWME was a key part of every company-wide meeting.

To help the values spread, we implemented a WOWME Awards program in which employees would nominate other employees for either wowing the customer, operating with urgency, working without mediocrity, making a positive wake, or engaging as an owner. We automated the nomination system using our CRM tool Salesforce.com. We put an annual amount of $20,000 into the awards pot and split the winnings between the employees who received at least three approved nominations for all five letters.

Entrepreneur Exercise: Define Your Company's Values

Time Needed: 5-8 Hours

Steps:
1. Gather your Management Team (or whole company depending on size) together for a full-day offsite. If it's just you or you and a partner, you can adjust this exercise appropriately.
2. Start by asking the group to each write down five values that most describe your culture and make your firm particularly unique.
3. Write down all of the values on a flip chart.
4. Group similar values together to come up with high level values. You can use the words underneath later in writing a couple sentence description of each value.
5. Get the list down to no more than 10 semi-finalists. Debate which ones should be on the list of 10 and which should not. Avoid generic values like "Be Ethical" or "Have Integrity," which every firm has.
6. Have each team member vote for the top three values they feel most represent your company, what it stands for, and what makes it unique.
7. Tally the votes and write down the top five on a new flip chart paper. Debate if these are the right five to be on the sheet. Resist the temptation to have more than five.
8. Work to turn your five final values into a memorable acronym by rearranging them and changing the wording but not the meaning of each value.

9. Make sure all your values are unique and memorable.
10. Roll-out your values and values acronym to your whole company and integrate your values into everything you do. Post them everywhere, include them in your performance review forms, and insert them into everyday language at the company.

Defining Your Vision and Mission

One of CEO's most important roles is to communicate the vision of the organization. This becomes even more important as the organization grows. If you have a vision but don't communicate it, you might as well not have a vision.

Once you get past the start-up phase when you're responsible for everything as "Chief Everything Officer", the six parts of the later stage CEO role become:

- Set Purpose, Mission, and Vision
- Define the Culture & Values
- Manage the Senior Leadership Team
- Oversee Resource Allocation (How money is spent)
- Communicate with Stakeholders (Employees, Board, Investors, Media, Partners, Community)
- Be a Customer Advocate

Creating a Clear Strategy That All Employees Know About

As you grow beyond 25 employees, you will find consistent employee communicating is one of the most important roles of CEO. It's no longer about the work you do, it's about the work of you dozens of employees being coordinated toward the same overarching clear goals. It's your job to make sure the direction the company is going in is clear and that all employees understand what it is your company is working on becoming the best in the world at.

At AA Global Sourcing Ltd we would hold an annual three-day retreat with our six persons Senior Leadership Team to set our objectives and plan for the year and then a quarterly 1 day off-site to set our targets for the upcoming quarter. We used a model called the One Page Strategic Plan that enabled our Senior Leadership Team to express our plans in a document that could be printed out on one sheet of paper. At each annual retreat we would update the left side of the plan and at each quarterly retreat we'd update the right side of the plan.

You can download the blank template we used for the one page strategy plan from a company called Gazelles. When we were finished, we have a meeting with the next-level down in the organization (which we called the Leadership Team) to gather feedback and then would distribute the document to all employees at the beginning of each quarter and hold a kickoff all-hands meetings to talk about the quarter or year's goals.

Putting in Place an Employee Handbook

Creating a single digital or printed manual that employees can refer to when they have questions about things like stock option plans, paid time off policies, and health benefits can be really helpful and save you and your fledgling HR department a lot of time. Try to document all the key policies and procedures you have and publish them annually in an Employee Handbook. Our employee handbook today contains the following sections:

1. Acceptable Use Policy
2. Attendance Policy
3. Badges Policy
4. Benefits Policy
5. Blogging Guidelines
6. Change of Information Policy
7. Community Giving Policy
8. Confidentiality Policy
9. Disability Leave
10. Dress Code Policy
11. Drug Policy
12. Ethics Policy
13. Employee Referral Policy
14. Family Medical Leave Policy
15. Food Policy
16. Freelancing Policy
17. Harassment/Professional Conduct Policy
18. Holidays Policy
19. Inclement Weather Policy
20. Internal Transfer Policy
21. Medical Leave
22. Paternity Leave
23. Maternity Leave
24. New Hire Forms Procedure
25. Paid Time Off (PTO) Policy
26. Payroll Procedure
27. Performance Evaluations
28. Phone Usage Policy
29. Printing Policy
30. Reimbursement/Purchase Requisition Procedure
31. Short Term Leave Policy
32. Supplier Policy
33. Travel & Entertainment Policy
34. Workers' Compensation Policy

Creating a Performance Review Process

As your organization grows, you'll eventually hire a full-time Director of HR and install what's called a Human Resources Information Systems (also known as a Human Resources Management System) that manages all aspects of HR including:

- Payroll
- Talent Management
- Recruiting
- Performance Reviews
- Total Rewards/Compensation

Eventually, you should implement a 360-degree performance review form. This form can be used for managers to get feedback from their peers and their staff members.

For now, you just need a basic performance review process in place. This can start with an Excel Spreadsheet or Microsoft Word document.

Part 2: Successful CEO

Chapter 7: Anyone Can Fill the Chief Executive Slot

Is there a certain blueprint to follow in order to attain this prestigious title? What professional and personal traits are necessary for the position? Technically, anyone can fill the chief executive slot, but typically those who have distinguished themselves in some manner and have strong leadership characteristics end up getting the job.

Education

There are no laws stipulating that chief executives must have attended college or that they must have a master's degree. However, very few people make it to the top of the corporate ladder these days without some sort of formal education.

Why is having a formal education so important? There is no simple answer to that question; however, completing university courses does provide one with exposure to a number of disciplines and causes a person to think, interact and share ideas with others, which are valuable experiences for a CEO to have. A degree from an Ivy League school or other top-tier institution is sometimes given even more credence because of the competitiveness that often accompanies such programs.

Many CEOs have some form of business degree. Note, however, that the degree could be in economics, management, finance or another business-related discipline. Some well-known chief executives, however, dropped out or never went to college.

- Richard Branson, CEO of Virgin Group.

- Michael Dell, CEO of Dell Computer (Nasdaq:DELL).
- Barry Diller, CEO of IAC/InterActiveCorp (Nasdaq:IACI).

Personality Traits

Having a degree from a top-notch school and an exceptional knowledge of the industry in which the company operates are great qualities to have. However, those qualities in and of themselves don't guarantee that a person will make it to the top of the corporate ladder. Personality traits may also play a role in an individual's ability to attain chief executive status. Typically, CEOs are:

- Good communicators, deal makers and managers.
- Extroverts who are eager to go out on the road and tell their company's story.
- Able and willing to present a cohesive vision and strategy to employees.
- Able to gain respect.

Jack Welch, former chairman and CEO of General Electric (NYSE:GE) is a great example of an extrovert who was able to gain respect, and who had a vision even as a low-level engineer at General Electric. While there, a higher-up took notice of his abilities, and the rest is history.

Experience

Generally speaking, a person must have a great deal of experience in the company's field in order to become CEO. A chief executive's job is to provide vision and a course for the company to navigate, which is difficult to do without extensive experience and a working knowledge of the potential risks and opportunities that lie ahead for the company.

Prior senior-level managerial experience is also generally a must. After all, how can an individual be expected to run a multimillion- or multibillion-dollar company with hundreds or thousands of employees unless he or she has previous experience managing and/or overseeing other employees?

A great example of someone who worked his way up the ranks is, again, Jack Welch. Welch joined General Electric in 1960 as an engineer and worked his way up to vice president and vice chairman before becoming CEO in 1981. By the time he got there, he knew the company and the landscape well. He had also previously held a high-level position.

Another example of a chief executive with a great deal of experience in his field is Eric Schmidt, former CEO of Novell and executive chairman of Google (Nasdaq:GOOG). Schmidt worked in research at Bell Labs early in his career. In addition, he served as chief technology officer at Sun Microsystems. These experiences helped him land his chief executive positions and become the success story he is today.

Then there's Andrea Jung, former CEO of Avon Products (NYSE:AVP). Jung has a sizable amount of experience in retail. After graduating from Princeton, she worked for Bloomingdales, where she was part of the management trainee program. From there, she also worked at Neiman Marcus, another high-end outfit where she served as executive vice president. When she finally came to Avon, she started as a consultant and then moved up to chief operating officer (COO) before finally landing the chief executive position.

Anne Mulcahy, former CEO of Xerox (NYSE:XRX), is another great of example of someone with a significant amount of experience in her field. In the mid-1970s, she started as a sales representative. She later worked as a vice president in human resources before climbing to senior vice president. All told, it was about 25 years before she became a chief executive; by that time, she knew the business extremely well.

The Bottom Line

Although some individuals are born leaders, most are made. Becoming a chief executive typically takes years of hard work. Extensive experience in the company's field is desirable and some companies tend to prefer those with degrees from upper-tier schools. Finally, those that have worked their way up from a low level within the organization may have an advantage, as they arguably know the company better than any outsider ever could.

Chapter 8: Making the Grade

Becoming a CEO doesn't happen overnight. CEOs work their way through the ranks and rise to the top ranks through a combination of hard work, perseverance, and traits and qualities that make him or her a top-notch business leader.

Get educated

If you want to be a CEO, you need to perform well in school. Ideally, you should complete both an undergraduate and a graduate degree. Focus your studies in an area that will be relevant to the industry you hope to enter, but keep things general enough that you can be flexible if you don't snag your dream job right out of University.

Many CEOs complete an undergraduate degree first, work for several years as an employee, rise through the ranks, and then return to an MBA program to earn a graduate degree. You don't need to put off joining the workforce just because you don't have all the education you want yet.

The larger the company you are hoping to one day rise to the top of, the more important it is that you attend (and graduate from) a school that has some cachet attached to its name. Obviously, some CEOs never even graduated college, but by the numbers, your best chance is to have a prestigious name on your degree. Consider Ivy League schools, of course, but don't forget smaller liberal arts colleges with respected business programs, either.

Spend extra time learning finances

Nothing helps a CEO make wise decisions for the company quite like a strong base of financial knowledge. While you can study and learn about finance and economics at any stage of your life, your college years are probably the best opportunity you will ever get. If you are not majoring in accounting, economics, or finance, take plenty of elective courses in those areas; even consider a minor.

Once you are a part of the workforce, take advantage of any and every opportunity your company offers to increase your financial knowledge with seminars, special classes, and other events. A great CEO never stops increasing, refreshing, or honing his or her knowledge.

Make connections early

During college, attend business seminars and networking events whenever you can. Apply to internships anywhere that you can show off your leadership skills and willingness to work hard; keep applying until you snag one (or more). Volunteer your time to help with charitable and other events that will allow you to rub shoulders with other future businesspeople. In short, act as though you are already climbing the corporate ladder before you even start.

Don't hesitate. It's never too early to start making the right impression on local business and civic leaders. You never know who might notice you and help smooth the way to your first real career job with a good reference or a kind word about you, when the time comes.

Shoot for the stars

As soon as you get a job based on your college qualifications (even if you are still in college at the time), treat it like you want to own the whole company. Employees who bring a sense of vitality and seriousness to their jobs are few and far between; be a company booster and a team player, and rest assured, you will be noticed. Accept extra tasks with zeal, and seek them out yourself whenever possible. Do everything you can to show your bosses that you are serious about advancing your professional life.

Do your utmost to get in touch with, and on friendly terms with, high-level executives in your business and wherever else you meet them during the course of your career. Observe the way they act and speak. You might even ask one to become a mentor for you. The worst that he or she can say is "no," and executives tend to appreciate brashness over propriety anyway. An executive mentorship, if you can get it, is a powerful tool for fast-tracking your career.

Stay flexible

It's not talked about too often these days, but raw ambition is a very useful (some might even say vital) trait for a business leader to possess. A part of being ambitious and aggressive about advancing your career is being open to taking paths you weren't expecting to take. At the very least, stay open to the possibility of switching shifts or locations in order to secure an advancement. If you jump at the chance to be a manager in a branch office somewhere far away, you will probably get the promotion over others who have reservations about it.

Once you've been with a company for a year or two, if you feel you are being passed over for advancement, scan job listings regularly and apply to any position that seems like a serious step up. A lot of CEOs started their careers as managers and junior vice presidents for two or three related businesses before becoming the head of their own company.

Don't be afraid to get entrepreneurial. CEOs and entrepreneurs share many traits, and a person planning to become one can get a great start by becoming the other. If you see an opportunity to go into business for yourself, and it seems like a better path to the executive level than your current one, don't hesitate to make the change. Cultivating a successful company from the ground up is an impressive distinction on any corporate resume.

Join a board. If you can, elect to become a member of the board of directors at a respectable company. This gives you valuable experience you can use to interact with the board at your own company once you become a CEO. It's also an excellent feather in your cap, as nearly half of all CEOs in the United States and United Kingdom served as board members at some point previous to becoming CEOs.

Chapter 9: Being a Great Chief Executive

Understand what a CEO does

The CEO of a company isn't necessarily the founder or even the owner; a CEO isn't quite the same thing as an entrepreneur. A CEO isn't a mere bookkeeper or office monkey, though, either. Rather, the CEO's job is to run the company; oversee financial decisions, resolve imbalances, and keep things on track for more profitability each and every year. This means a great CEO is a combination of an ideas person (like an entrepreneur), willing to take risks and think big; and a hands-on person, eagle-eyed in matters of money and human resources, always willing to dig into the details until everything is perfect.

Rely on experience

Most CEOs attain their position after many years; sometimes decades in the same industry, or even at the same company. Once you reach the top, don't forget your roots. Use all that you know about your business (or area of business) to run it as efficiently as possible; differences between written policy and practical "ground rules;" connections who can give you insight into places you are no longer closely connected to; attitudes and beliefs among low-level employees about the business.

Lead with vision

To be a truly great CEO, you must exercise control over your company by shaping the workplace environment to be one that has a distinct and palpable culture. In other words, a great leader creates a sense among his or her employees that they are a part of something truly special, something bigger and more significant than any one part of the whole. Your attitude and actions towards your workforce very clearly set the tempo at every level of the company.

Demand the world of your workers, but allow them to make mistakes. Show them that the company believes in them enough to let them keep trying until they make it; as long as they are good enough at their jobs to make it in a big way when they do. Encourage productivity by encouraging risk-taking and personal judgment calls. You always have the last word if something is a poor fit for the business.

Be clear-cut

As a CEO, it's your job to run the entire business. Though you delegate many of the daily tasks to your subordinates, you are the one with the bird's-eye view who can see the whole pattern of the company as it breathes and changes over time. Bearing that in mind, use what you see and know to communicate your plans and explain your decisions to your workers clearly, plainly, and openly. If they know what your vision for the company is, they will have a much easier time helping you to realize that vision.

Stay connected

Never succumb to the illusion that the CEO lives and works in an ivory tower while the rest of the business goes on below, guided by distant edicts from on high. An effective CEO is always in the thick of things; visiting every department, assisting with any task he or she is qualified to assist with, speaking to employees and listening to their feedback. A part of your time is necessarily spent at the top, planning ahead and thinking in broad terms, but the rest of your time should be spent in the thick of the action.

Feel free to micromanage if you need to show someone the way you did prefer them to do something. Don't simply berate them or tell them what they are doing wrong; instead, clear them out of the driver's seat and do it yourself, explaining the reasoning of every step and action along the way. A great CEO leads by example, not insult.

Embody strategy

Above all else, once you become a CEO, your business is the future of the company. You must be adept at thinking six moves ahead, seeing around the next corner, and guessing what the future will hold. Stay abreast of trends and always think about your company's place in the business world at large. How can you stay king of the hill? If you are not, how can you knock the others out of the top spot? If these are the questions that help guide your business strategy, you will be the most effective CEO you can be.

Chapter 10: CEO's Guide to Communication Skill

CEO is the leader of the business and as such, is expected to be an excellent communicator. This means more than just being eloquent, it means delivering meaningful content as well. The effective use of language is a challenging skill which many of us poorly develop as we go through school (or so our teachers would tell us). But proper use of language will go a long way to influence people to get the things done that are important to the business.

In a business setting, people are prepared to forgive communication deficiencies when using a second language but mostly expect some level of correctness when using your native language. Given that many young businesses are founded by entrepreneurs with primarily technical backgrounds who can communicate well-enough to get the business going (and perhaps funded), few are appropriate to be the guest speaker at a CEO conference. For the entrepreneur to remain in CEO role, it is important to develop effective communication skills to meet the demands of the job.

CEO needs to be able to communicate the essence of the business strategy and equally important, the methodology for achieving it. CEO needs to be approachable; every encounter should be a memorable one, even at the coffee machine. CEO is expected to be able to receive critical input and understand how to deliver critical output without being offensive. CEO is expected to be able to run a meeting efficiently, illustrating how to respect time. CEO is expected to understand when positive contribution is being made and so recognize it. CEO is expected to be able to stand in front of the team and deliver motivating presentations (and show how to be brief). CEO is expected to be able to lead sales calls, develop partner relationships, discuss pricing and deflate critical support situations. CEO needs to be able to use communication skills for many things.

Not everyone is born with the capability to be an excellent communicator; in fact, few people seem to have this as a natural skill. It does not mean you will fail in taking on CEO role, it means you have to work hard to be an effective communicator and more importantly, understand how to use the team around you to compensate for any weaknesses. This chapter addresses the many aspects of communication CEO should be aware of as well as a variety of ways communication skills can be improved. It should be no surprise, that practice does make perfect in this instance, but even endless practice will not turn a poor communicator into an eloquent one, especially in spontaneous scenarios.

Establishing Communication Rhythm

Communication is a challenging aspect of business behaviour that is rarely perfected. In fact, you should never become complacent about communication always striving to use communication as a way to better integrate teams working together. One of the most effective ways to plan communication is through a defined rhythm; making communication predictable in terms of the who, what, where, when and why people will hear things from CEO, in this case.

Predictable communication sounds easy at first glance; but over time it can fall into the background as noise that people don't pay attention to. It is important that the content be fresh, ideally interactive when appropriate and most importantly contain value to everyone listening (that is the hard part). The benefit of rhythm is that the team comes to expect and anticipate certain opportunities to connect with CEO. It reduces the feeling that no communication is happening; it increases the comfort that the team will be kept informed authoritatively. It reduces the impact on rumours.

Here are some ideas about the types of rhythm to establish from the office of CEO

1. Annual presentation of the strategic plan

A great presentation to hold at a team-wide kick-off at the start of a fiscal year. The materials should present the strategy at a high level and contain information about how the company is executing against it. It should identify relevant challenges and objectives and be honest on how things are going so far. Everyone should be able to relate to the challenges of the Company not just sales (targets) and development (product deliverables). The materials should be available for anyone to look at throughout the year. Elements of the plan should also be presented to all new employees as part of their in-take process; ideally presented personally by CEO.

2. Quarterly results

For young companies, the team typically likes to hear CEO present results. It allows people to ask questions of the business leader, which increases confidence overall (depending on the answers of course). It also provides a forum for CEO to ask questions of the team which improves the feeling of equality that many modern team structures thrive on. No secrets is a good policy although couching answers may sometimes be needed. Not everyone can take direct and honest answers in an open forum like a team-wide meeting.

3. Company milestone announcements

Not always rhythm oriented in terms of time frame, but predictable in terms of making sure everyone knows of the achievements as they occur. The most common ones would include a large account win (or revenue achievement), but the ones that recognize some of the little things also help such as passing through a total lead count goal, number of active customers, closing the Nth support call, etc. Sometimes the leader of the relevant operational area will make these announcements and then CEO will follow up as appropriate. It depends on whether there is risk CEO would seem out-of-touch by not appearing to know about the achievement until the operational manager announces it. The operational manager will feel slighted that they can't announce a key achievement in their area; communication is not easy!

4. Monthly internal newsletter

Not that commonly done per say, but CEO could issue via email a personally written update about important or interesting items that affect the Company. It might contain contributions from others in the Company; include a summary of recent announcements, etc. Marketing might get involved to help prepare it so it has the appropriate shine.

5. Recognizing individual achievement

Like many aspects of communication, it can be a double-edged sword. Who do you recognize, how much do you say, how do you know if you are leaving someone out? Do you exaggerate your knowledge of the event or your familiarity with the person (perhaps larger company issue)? Nonetheless, knowing that CEO will recognize special achievement helps people strive for special achievement.

A subtlety to keep in mind is even though something is communicated, it does not mean everyone has heard it. Sometimes people are absent or do not have time to attend the communication event (or can't hear it because it is not broadcast clearly (a common problem for remote office workers)) others did not appreciate the written delivery of a message (e.g. yet another email) so are also looking for the achievement to be recognized the next time the team meets more formally. Don't hesitate to repeat certain messages using a variety of communication methods (email, video or audio conference, post on internal web, hang message in lunch room, etc) sometimes just the repetitiveness helps (or hinders). Winning at communication is not easy.

Perception of Excellence

Setting a high standard for effective communication is an important element of being CEO. If you don't check spelling or grammar, why should anyone else? If you are not prepared with your speech, why should the team act any differently? If you can't form a proper sentence in a public setting the embarrassment for everyone else may be too much. It may all sound obvious, but requires a bit of extra time to do well so surprisingly does not get done as often as one would think.

Some obvious hints in the right direction include:

Always use the spell checker to validate outgoing email. There is nothing more embarrassing than sending an email with gross spelling or grammatical errors. If you receive one, take the time to tell the sender how unacceptable it is to send email without spell checking. Bad grammar and spelling distract from the message; really!

Have a trusted source review important communication prior to sending. It's rarely the case that the author is the best reviewer. This means you have to leave time for the reviewing cycle so keep that in mind.

Review formal presentations, especially if created in tools like Microsoft PowerPoint. It is embarrassing to be unfamiliar with animation or slide timing or to be caught off guard with a theme you are not familiar with, especially in front of prospective customers. Never blame the slide creator, if you are presenting, they are your slides.

If proper communication rhythm is established, the time needed to achieve a degree of excellence can be planned in. If communication is often ad hoc, it's hard to have it all come out right.

Practicing

If you are one of those who feel uncomfortable with communication, practicing helps. Some straightforward (and hopefully somewhat safe) venues and methods include:

Make a small speech during a team lunch. It provides a forum to practice standing in front of an audience appearing to sound prepared (even if nervous). Make sure you look at the people you are presenting to, make sure you ask questions and take a few questions. The more comfortable you feel interacting with an audience, the better.

Review what you are presenting. This is especially true with formalized slide presentations. It is very embarrassing to be in the middle of an important customer presentation and have problems with slide mechanics. Ask someone to come to your office for a dry run; rehearse overall timing of presentation and what key messages you want to give for each slide. Make sure the slides are properly checked for spelling, grammar and formatting errors.

Be purposeful with all emails. As many people would say, email is perhaps one of the worst used forms of communication available. No structure, no personality, easy for someone to convey messages in tones that were not intended. Given that an email from CEO is an important email, it should be well written, to the point, use language properly and be clear as to what follow ups are required. Don't be one of those who always do a Reply-All, rarely checks spelling or grammar and have no specific point to make. If needed, have someone review a company-wide email before it is sent, or put it in Draft for a day and re-read the next day to see if it still says what you intend.

In the end, you'll likely find you are not as poor a communicator as you may think. Your passion for the business tends to uplift the way in which you talk about it which will come across when communicating. The important thing is to be prepared, take your time and use the team around you to illustrate your ability to get the message across.

Communicating with Customers

For the most part, customers would not often have a chance to meet with CEO of a Company. As such, you should treat the opportunity with equal respect and use as many skills as you can to make sure the customer finds the encounter the strongest reason yet to do business with you. You need to establish a variety of things when communicating with customers:

Mutual respect: Regardless of the position of the person you meet with, they are an influencer over a business decision. Treat everyone with maximum respect; make sure they relish the encounter with you. Refer to them by name, inquire about their job activities, other relevant experiences including and especially any exposure to the competition. If they have used your solution, get some feedback. Feedback given to CEO is the best feedback possible, users tend to focus on high level needs not the nit-picky stuff they might tell a product manager or support specialist.

Mind your sales manners: It's easy to always be in selling mode to the point where your audience tires of the incessant pushing on differentiators and value propositions. Once you feel you have the sales close you need, focus on the partnership being established. Assume they are becoming a customer; as a given, so use the time to make sure they become a long-lasting customer. Let your sales team get them across the finish line, your job is largely to give the customer a reason to jump across the line to the benefits that being a customer would bring.

Be approachable but careful: Every CEO hands out business cards with contact information. Call me any time statements are easily made in the heat of a business meeting. What are you going to do if the customer does indeed call you or send you an email? The key thing is to provide rapid response and thoughtful follow up. The impression left on a customer where CEO actually responds to communication is very positive. Few customers will abuse this and if they do, your team is there to step in and take up the mantle as needed. Don't forget your team should not be cut out of the loop so always try to redirect the contact to the appropriate team member but make sure they respond as well or it looks like you are just shuffling the customer off to a corner.

Follow up: If you say you will do something, make sure you do. One of the most common follow-up faux pas relates to product issues where the customer mentions a deficiency and CEO says it will be checked into. Does it get checked into; even if the answer is yes, does the customer know this? Make sure that some communication is sent to the customer to indicate you have followed up even if all you say is that you are working on it. An important issue to a customer occupies their thoughts every day whereas it may only be a fleeting thought amongst many for you.

The role of CEO will certainly put you in touch with customers regularly (it should). You need to be prepared, well practiced and confident. You are the business leader and the customer wants to feel they are being led down the right path for their business needs.

Chapter 11: Deciding What to Delegate

As your company grows, you will be forced to delegate more responsibility to the members of your staff. Here is how to decide what to delegate and what to tackle yourself.

In the early stages of your company you are not just CEO. Your roles include accountant, head of human resources, and customer service representative to name a few. But as you grow and hire more people, it falls to them as much as to you to make your company a success.

In the case of small businesses, the founder will often have a hard time relinquishing the complete control they experienced before they had a staff. CEOs of small businesses are "so busy just doing the day-to-day stuff, they don't step back and think, 'You know what, I could make this a lot easier for myself and get better results for my business if I only delegate it," says CEO of a company I use to work with.

The more you can successfully delegate, the more time you will have to spend on the challenges that only you can navigate for your company. Or as I always put it, delegating "frees up the top person to do their strategic thinking and make sure the big picture's being addressed." But it can still be tricky to know what to delegate, who to hire so you can delegate with ease, and how to check in on the people you have delegated to; this chapter will tell you how.

Some tasks are readily delegated because they require little creative interpretation. Phone calls, paperwork, and even bills and finances are often unloaded hastily onto new hires or outsourced to contractors. Delegating administrative tasks is the first thing everybody thinks of because they hate to do it themselves.

Still that is no reason to skimp on those aspects of your business. Successful companies put a premium on customer service and as a result, they hire and train their employees in a very specific way to make what could be a rote task, answering customer e-mails and phone calls, a dynamic interaction that ultimately helps the companies' bottom lines.

But not all tasks have a deeper meaning; some just need to be checked off a list as complete or incomplete. Not delegating these types of tasks can waste your precious time. For example a company that collects business performance data for medical practitioners that struggled to delegate at the right time. The company, which employs 20 people, had a major event that was a financial linchpin for them. Understandably given its importance, they figured they should put one of their top executives on it, however putting on the event is almost all operational and easily delegated downward if they only trusted their people or thought it through how they could break the work down.

So what is a good rule for when to delegate?

Think about whether a seemingly simple task can take on an extra dimension that would improve your business. If the answer is no, get your assistant on the phone. If it's yes, roll up your sleeves.

What Can't You Afford to Delegate

Business owners are much more hesitant to delegate strategic and creative assignments because they often have a strong vision for just how those projects should turn out.

But stepping back from the details, even in the case of a more creative project, can be a good thing. You have to know and value the fact that the person you delegate to is not always going to make the same decision that you would make because otherwise there is no point in having the task delegated.

We have seen the value of delegating creative tasks firsthand. CEO of Economic Modelling Specialists, a company that collects employment data and provides economic analyses for colleges and universities, was approached by his marketing manager about rebranding the company, particularly its Web presence.

The manager and his team ended up doing a stellar job, boosting the company's visibility, and the CEO admits that, though he was nervous about ceding control of such a big strategic project at first, if he had tried to micromanage it, or if I had tried to really ride the details of it, it would not have gone so well. So what projects does CEOs handle himself? Big picture planning and the top echelons of new endeavours, such as forming high-level partnerships.

Matching an Employee's Tasks with Their Pay

Another important tenet of delegation is to dole out responsibility in such a way that you pair a task with people who have the right talents and are in the right pay bracket.

83

You don't want your $100 an hour employee doing the work a $12 an hour employee could handle, do you?

Well that is the conventional wisdom but a CEO we work with handles customer support along with his engineers and people give him funny looks for it. "When I tell people that, they look at me like I am smoking crack," he told me. "They say, 'why would you pay an engineer $150,000 to answer phones when you could pay someone $8 an hour?' If you make the engineers answer e-mails and phone calls from the customers, the second or third time they get the same question, they will actually stop what they are doing and fix the code. Then we don't have those questions anymore. Still unless there is some added benefit of having employees with higher salaries tackle seemingly menial tasks, it is best to assign work with pay grade in mind.

Hiring the Right People

Smaller companies are often more flexible so you would think they would have the inside track when it came to delegating, but the opposite can actually be the case. At a large company, the roles and responsibilities are often parsed out very specifically, but in a smaller company, the work is shared so much. Somebody may wear a hat today and then tomorrow they are going to be doing another type of work, and so it's less clear who is completely capable and comfortable in any one thing because so much of it is shared.

Still if you have a staff that you trust, you can rely on them to help propel the company forward. But what exactly does it mean to trust your staff? Trust obviously comes in a lot of different ways. The person that babysits my kids, I trust them, but they don't necessarily share my business vision. However, even in the case of your employees, when you have faith in their skills and abilities, it's not always the same as a shared worldview or vision for the company. One of the real challenges of building management teams early on in the evolution of an organization is to ensure the right balance of commonality and diversity. You want people to have enough common ground to communicate easily and yet have varied perspectives to avoid groupthink. Below are some traits to look for in new hires to make your job easier.

What Traits in Employees Make Delegating a Breeze?

One way to handle the issue of trust is to only hire people you know well. Many companies will hire friends, family members, and former colleagues in the early stages of company building because there is more reason there to believe that they will be coming at problems with a similar set of approaches and a similar set of values.

Unfortunately, this is a luxury a CEO can only afford while his or her company is small. But you could tap into a network of business contacts, customers, vendors, and partners, which you could frequently call on to get the scoop on a job candidate. A CEO we know once said that "he once discovered from a customer that he had known for years that an applicant was very intelligent, but rested on his intellectual laurels and didn't have a good work ethic".

Once you have the potential employee in the hot seat, here are some characteristics you should look for that make it easier to delegate tasks once they come on board.

A friend of mine looks for people who are quick on the uptake, not just for learning to perform tasks, but so that they can internalize the company's mission and vision. "Everybody on my team is somebody I might delegate to," he said. Since he often hands out tasks that require cooperation, he looks for hires that are respectful of other people.

You need an employee who isn't afraid to ask questions, or in a pinch to ask for help, to make delegating a success. Look for people who are independent, but not like cowboy mentality where they are going to run with something all by themselves off into the fields ahead of the rest of us. Look for a person who takes ownership of a task and takes the initiative to make it successful.

Communicate Clearly

Delegating requires a lot of thought by the person giving the assignment, in part because you always need to be more explicit than your gut instinct or common sense suggests. Make sure there is no room for error or misinterpretation. When you meet with the employee to delegate the work you should let them know here is exactly what I want you to do, here is my expectations, here is how we are going to touch base with each other to make sure you are comfortable doing it and that I am comfortable with how you are doing it.

You also need to make yourself available for plenty of questions. If you give off the impression that you don't want to be bothered, the person will pick up on that and potentially walk away with an incomplete understanding of the assignment.

Getting the Most Out of Part-Time Employees

It is particularly important to communicate clearly with your part-time employees because they have a different mental, emotional, and sometimes physical relationship with your company. If you employ a lot of part-time people due to your line of work; this can complicate the delegation process. They are not thinking about your company when they are not billing you, so they are not going to step up and think about things that I haven't thought about first.

Unless you tasks them with being creative and makes it part of the job description, contract employees won't do more or less than what you tells them to do explicitly. This lesson can even carry over to your full-time employees. You have to hold in mind how they conceptualize your company. If you keep their personal and professional goals in mind, for example who is looking to expand their skill set, when assigning tasks, you can make them more motivated and potentially get better results because of the enthusiasm they are more likely to bring to tasks they have a proclivity towards.

Following Up

Depending on the size of your company and the type of work you do, you will want to check up with the people you have delegated tasks to at different intervals. We recommend a minimum of once a week; holds weekly and biweekly meetings with different members of your staff. It's important to remember that these sessions are not opportunities to tamper with all the details of the project but rather to determine if it's more generally headed in the right direction. A CEO we use to work with always explains to his employees that the check-ins are not resultant of a lack of trust. He says, "I am going to be monitoring you, but not because I think you are going to do poor work, it's because I want to do everything I can to make sure that you do excellent work.

Chapter 12: The Role of an Executive Director of a Non-profit Organization

Non-profit organizations are structured in a slightly different way than for-profit businesses, although there are a few similarities.

The makeup and duties of a Non-profit's executive management team, for example, is similar to for-profit companies in a number of ways. An executive director sits in the top spot in a Non-profit organization, and performs a range of duties similar to those of chief executive officers in corporate businesses. Understanding the role of an executive director of a Non-profit organization can shed light into how Non-profits function on the inside.

Working with the Board

An experienced board of directors can provide strategic guidance, valuable contacts and resources to Non-profit organizations. While the board of directors is responsible for making a range of vital company decisions, it is not involved in making day-to-day operational decisions. As the most senior manager in the operational hierarchy, one of an executive director's main roles is to act as a liaison between the board of directors and the rest of the organization. Executive directors meet with the board regularly to keep them informed on operational issues and work with them to come up with strategic solutions to complex challenges.

Management Role

Executive directors oversee the heads of each department in a Non-profit, including marketing, fundraising, program development, HR management and accounting. Executive directors can also oversee one or more lower-level executives in larger organizations.

Department leaders look to the director for strategic guidance in their areas. The executive director leads the fundraising department in setting annual income goals, for example, and works with program development managers to set standards for serving the organization's targeted needs groups. The smaller a Non-profit organization is, the more directly involved the director is likely to be in each departmental function. In the smallest Non-profits, for example, an executive director may handle all accounting duties and half of the fundraising duties, in addition to executive-level duties.

Public Relations

Executive directors fulfil vital roles outside the office and after normal business hours. Directors are expected to attend and possibly host a range of fundraising events, new program inaugurations and public relations events. Directors often speak directly with reporters, donors, government representatives and members of the community at these events, spending a good deal of time acting as the public face of the organization.

Executive directors must keep a spotless personal reputation because of the additional scrutiny, which is not always the case in for-profit businesses. A personal scandal in the life of an executive director can tarnish a Non-profit's reputation for years. In a way, a director has to consider himself on duty at all time as a representative of the organization.

Company Liaison

In addition to appearing at official events, executive directors act as a liaison between their organizations and a range of external stakeholders. Directors develop and maintain relationships with other Non-profit leaders, for example, looking for opportunities to partner with other organizations to serve good causes. Directors also work personally with leaders in the business and government world, cultivating long-term strategic partnerships or donor relationships to increase the organization's effectiveness serving unmet needs.

Chapter 13: CEO's Guide to Corporate Human Resources

In the last five years, more and more CEOs have recognized the strategically critical role the human resources function plays in many of the issues they face, including mergers and acquisitions, corporate restructurings, talent management, increased board oversight, and new governance and reporting requirements. In response, many forward-thinking chief executives are making structural changes to how HR fits within their organizations and significantly raising the bar regarding what they expect from their HR leaders.

To better understand how that move is unfolding and its implications for senior HR executives, we conducted in-depth interviews with nine CEOs who are leading the way in leveraging human resources in their organizations, to find out how they are aligning human resources with business objectives and what their expectations are of their HR leaders. Based on those expectations, our competency-based research and our consulting experience, we identified the skill sets needed to succeed in this more demanding environment. Finally, we examined the competency profiles of 100 top human resources leaders to assess the readiness of the existing talent pool in the face of these new requirements.

A combination of forces puts the focus on HR

Human resources' elevated place on CEO agenda is due to the convergence of two factors unfolding simultaneously in the global business arena. First, well-documented demographic shifts the aging of the workforce, global economic expansion, a heightened demand for tech-savvy workers and a decrease in employee loyalty are making the successful identification and retention of talent more difficult than ever and a powerful source of competitive advantage for those who can do it well.

The cost of labour and benefits is horrific and there are increasing liabilities for all companies that employ large numbers of people. How do you stay competitive? How do you treat your people right? How do you get people who want to work for you? How do you not bankrupt your financials by doing it?

That's an important challenge for HR.

Second, boards are acutely aware that many of the issues for which they have oversight from acquisition strategy to succession planning succeed or fail based on the quality of the people involved. Organizations that have the highest-quality and highest-calibre members on their team are the ones that are going to win. Either one of these two factors would be enough to put human resources on the boardroom agenda. The combination, however, results in a talent supply and demand unbalance that is causing corporate leaders in all sectors to rethink this function.

That rethinking begins with the job description of the HR leader. Gone are the days when the role was defined by the minutiae of recordkeeping, benefits administration and the establishment of a vaguely understood corporate culture.

CEOs want the HR leaders. "HR executives should realize that they become valuable members of the executive committee and have earned a seat at the table not just by recruiting and retaining talent. HR has to play a more proactive role and not a reactive role. Of course, these new demands are in addition to, rather than replacements for, the traditional skills and capabilities that have long been expected of HR executives. HR leader have to be brilliant in the management of human capital and be very savvy in the ways of business. That's a tall order.

New competencies for new opportunities

In order to assess how the competencies of the current crop of HR leaders stood up against these new standards, we examined the competency profiles of more than 100 senior HR executives assessed over the past six years. Results indicate that while HR executives tended to score higher in interpersonal skills when compared with a pool of executives across all functions, they scored lower on strategic vision, business acumen and global orientation confirming that HR executives have significant catching up to do if they are to meet the requirements for a seat at the senior management table.

A culture that supports HR's strategic role

CEOs recognize it is not merely a question of asking their HR leaders to rise to the challenge of new capabilities and responsibilities. If they want HR to deliver at a higher level, they have to create the environment that allows that to happen.

Historically, there's been an issue where the HR person is the lowest member of the senior team and not a peer. Right off the bat, you have got a problem. You need someone who can carry themselves as an equal. Corporate chiefs are employing a range of strategies to shake up such outmoded thinking. At

The New York Times Company, for example, The organization was restructured to accelerate a change in the culture, to increase accountability and to improve the goal-setting process, that restructuring, which included expanding the Executive Committee, created disciplined HR initiatives that were led by the senior-level executives of the company. These initiatives were designed to drive performance and innovation and advance the company's transition to a multi-platform media company.

A company we work with few years ago made head of HR a direct report to the CEO and an integral member of the 10-person Operating Group that manages the company on a day-to-day basis. They also moved HR leader just a few doors down from CEO's office and in close proximity to the other senior executives.

"You have to foster the communication," The CEO explains. "The other senior members of the team have to appreciate the value that is brought by the head of HR."

Another engineering company we work with has successfully integrated HR leader and the HR function. "I've been privileged in my last three positions to not only select the person in that spot but also to create the management structure around it," the CEO said. "In doing that, I have made the person not just an HR professional but created an organizational structure and an expectation that that person participates as a full business partner." In fact, "Every unit has a business partner from HR on its management team. We deploy them through our units," he adds.

CEO of another Hi-Tech company we worked with also stresses the importance of integrating HR into the various business units within the company. "HR isn't a floor or a bunch of offices. It sits with the business groups. Each business group has a generalist HR person who is an integral part of their strategy.

As at many companies, the talent review process at the company is driven by the firm's HR leader. Critically, however, it is not siloed in HR but central to the firm's strategic planning. We are two years into a talent identification and succession planning process where we assess and discuss the talent two to three levels below me across all of our lines of business, says the CEO. Each line of business talks about their people in talent review discussions with other lines of business so we know our talent more broadly, understand our collective bench strength and can move talent across lines as necessary to meet business needs. We also do succession planning three levels into the company within the lines of business.

However the elevation of the HR profile occurs, it requires a commitment from the top. Setting the tone about development as a CEO is everything, "A lot of people talk about that, but most companies don't have an explicit commitment from senior management to make their people better. And that is part of the contract here". Said the CEO. That commitment must also include the financial backing to support the success of HR in attracting, retaining and compensating top talent.

Solving a talent shortage

Not surprisingly, the demand for HR leaders meeting this stringent set of requirements far outstrips the supply. Appropriately, forward-thinking companies are finding that the solution lies in making the silos between departments more permeable. Promising HR executives are rotated out into line positions in sales, marketing or operations; returning to their home departments with a broader perspective, they codify and institutionalize their knowledge and thus bolster the HR talent pipeline. At the same time, some organizations are bringing in executives from sales, finance or marketing to take HR leadership roles, betting that they can get up to speed on domain-specific knowledge while leveraging their business perspective.

The latter approach has been used successfully at a medical device company we work with recently. They take an operating executive of enormous potential and put them in a key HR role somewhere in the organization and allow them an opportunity to develop and mature from that position. It brings you immediately into the inner sanctum, and you learn what is really happening, who knows what and who the key people are. And when you roll back out to run a business, you have some additional skills.

HR leaders who have worked at companies that have gone through monumental transitions have a lot to offer. I think you are advantaged when you attract people who enjoy rolling up their sleeves and view their positions as being agents of change.

I think transitions can bring out the best in HR professionals when they are willing and eager to step up to the challenges. They should view themselves as critical leaders in the change process.

Seizing the opportunity

While a rapidly shifting and complex business environment is forcing talent management to the top of CEO agenda, those CEOs are responding by driving change in a function that has been historically relegated to second-class status. They are elevating the HR function to give it full membership in the inner circle and are raising expectations accordingly.

HR leaders with the full complement of skills and perspectives necessary for success are in short supply, causing companies to develop innovative strategies for identifying candidates for positions that will not wait. At the same time, the human resources profession needs to apply its expertise to itself expanding its skill sets, establishing best practices and developing a culture of knowledge sharing to successfully grasp this opportunity and in that challenging transition, CEO may be HR's biggest advocate.

If the HR person has a wealth of knowledge of the capabilities of the organization; there are a hundred things they can bring to the table because they are, in many ways, the central nervous system of the company. They are the eyes and the ears. They are great observers. So they are often aware of issues, problems and roadblocks ahead of the people in the room. And if you listen to them, I think you can make much more intelligent decisions around the human assets in a corporation.

If you believe that leading and managing your people is the most important thing you do, then not only does HR have to be at your table, it has to be at your right hand!

Chapter 14: Rescuing Your Corporate Culture

Immediately following a round of layoffs in early December of 2008, a young manager with great potential and a decade of experience with responsibility for a team of over 100 in the mutual fund service centre had his door closed mid-morning as call volume built during another volatile day on Wall Street. The Divisional Head of Human Resources at one of our long-standing clients recounted that she was surprised at this, immediately assuming that he was out sick that day. She opened the door, and, to her surprise, the manager was sitting at his desk working. Asked why he was not, in his characteristic style, more visible to the team at this critical juncture, he replied, "The layoffs earlier in the week have everyone on the team very upset. I just figured it would be best to lie low...you know, wait for the dust to settle. I will get out next week after our Monday staff meeting when the air has cleared a little bit."

Needless to say, the HR director sprang into action to rescue the situation, organizing an informal town hall meeting at the close of business that day, followed by daily breakfast meetings with smaller segments of the team over the next week. The manager committed to hour-long one-on-one sessions with every team leader before the holidays.

The current business climate requires a significant culture change for many financial services firms and there is no greater challenge in any area of business. It is a time-leadership behaviour practices. Better leadership starts with clear, transparent, repetitive, compelling and honest communications with all employees on mission, strategy, tasks, metrics and rewards. Only this type of prolonged, direct communication will build "cultural glue" through better alignment, reinforced using intangible rewards that will allow teams and firms to excel in a down market.

As financial services firms continue to go through the painful process of deleveraging their balance sheets and financial expectations, there is a concurrent deleveraging of the organizational management structure underway; senior managers are required to spend more time "leading" as opposed to "doing." The leadership of a firm that recognizes this fact and responds with the appropriate time and effort to replace tangible with intangible rewards has the opportunity to significantly outperform competitors through higher morale, better performance under duress, lower turnover and improved alignment with strategies and goals.

For several decades, most financial services firms, particularly large global banks and investment businesses, have experienced significant growth while maintaining extraordinary operating margins. This has allowed them to adopt aggressive, tangible pay practices to reward performers, and to take a "shortcut" verses investing the time to build a more sophisticated, intangible motivation and reward systems. This "shortcut" has permitted senior managers at multiple levels to expect more from employees and hold down turnover, while simultaneously allowing the managers themselves to spend a much larger percentage of their own time in the pursuit of "doing" instead of "leading." In the investment business, this meant finding clients and generating superior investment returns, as opposed to spending time face-to-face with employees. As a result, the "cultural glue" that binds many financial firms is disproportionately weighted to excess compensation.

As the industry enters a prolonged period of contraction, we will experience three to five years of significantly slower growth and lower profitability, which will be essential in replacing or augmenting the "money" culture that dominated previous years. The lack of coaching and mentoring by a manager leaves employees feeling isolated and uncertain. Furthering this concern, compensation is falling significantly which greatly impacts lifestyles of the more senior employees. If the culture of the firm does not respond to fill the gaps in leadership following the departure of these senior members, employee misbehaviour and turnover will present significant enterprise risk management issue. Understanding the success of the cultures and motivation systems of other organizations with much lower margins and rates of historic growth such as airlines, hotels, and manufacturing, best practices in culture building can be quickly identified as highly successful without resorting to extraordinary financial rewards.

These include:

- Frequent, consistent contact between staff and senior management (daily, weekly);
- Clearly defined metrics for performance that are transparent to all members of the team (daily, weekly);
- Regular and honest benchmarking against internal performance targets (monthly, quarterly);
- Extensive training to provide employees with the tools necessary to deliver against the tasks required (mandatory multiple weeks a year), and;
- Frequent efforts to recognize and reward superior performance by both individuals and teams, allowing the team to focus on small wins, rather than despair

on broader market challenges and risks (weekly, monthly).

The time-consuming nature of these initiatives, even if only a few are utilized, is significant when compared to the half hour reviews at bonus time that occur once a year at many firms. The actual range of tools for building intangible rewards is almost endless and well-documented in business academic literature as well as in the leadership practices of best-in-class competitors like General Electric.

This significant investment of time "leading" on the part of managers at every level will set a tone of upbeat momentum and will penetrate into the market with competitors and clients. There is no doubt that most employees are motivated to do a good job by the intellectual stimulation and recognition of good work, as much as by the money, and this is widely proven in surveys. The culture change will occur as managers replace a larger portion of the reward system from tangible financial rewards to intangible psychic gratification through social reinforcement. Managers must sacrifice a portion of their time in "production" to make this happen. It is a valuable undertaking in and of itself, worthy of rewards comparable to those usually associated with business production. CEO and Division Executives must reinforce to all managers that spending time "leading" is just as valuable as "doing." Every manager must step up and contribute to the business of building culture; sending the message to subordinates and peers that this deleveraging of the organizational structure is the only way to rescue the corporate culture in this difficult and complex market environment.

Chapter 15: CEO's Guide to Corporate Finance

It's one thing for a Chief Finance Officer (CFO) to understand the technical methods of valuation and for members of the finance organization to apply them to help line managers monitor and improve company performance. But it's still more powerful when CEOs, board members, and other nonfinancial executives internalize the principles of value creation. Doing so allows them to make independent, courageous, and even unpopular business decisions in the face of myths and misconceptions about what creates value.

When an organization's senior leaders have a strong financial compass, it's easier for them to resist the siren songs of financial engineering, excessive leverage, and the idea (common during boom times) that somehow the established rules of economics no longer apply. Misconceptions like these which can lead companies to make value-destroying decisions and slow down entire economies take hold with surprising and disturbing ease.

What we hope to do in this chapter is show how four principles, or cornerstones, can help senior executives and board members make some of their most important decisions. The four cornerstones are disarmingly simple:

1.   The core-of-value principle establishes that value creation is a function of returns on capital and growth, while highlighting some important subtleties associated with applying these concepts.

2. The conservation-of-value principle says that it doesn't matter how you slice the financial pie with financial engineering, share repurchases, or acquisitions; only improving cash flows will create value.

3. The expectations treadmill principle explains how movements in a company's share price reflect changes in the stock market's expectations about performance, not just the company's actual performance (in terms of growth and returns on invested capital). The higher those expectations, the better that company must perform just to keep up.

4. The best-owner principle states that no business has an inherent value in and of itself; it has a different value to different owners or potential owners; a value based on how they manage it and what strategy they pursue.

View these principles and their implications at a glance

Ignoring these cornerstones can lead to poor decisions that erode the value of companies. Consider what happened during the run-up to the financial crisis that began in 2007. Participants in the securitized-mortgage market all assumed that securitizing risky home loans made them more valuable because it reduced the risk of the assets. But this notion violates the conservation-of-value rule. Securitization did not increase the aggregated cash flows of the home loans, so no value was created, and the initial risks remained. Securitizing the assets simply enabled the risks to be passed on to other owners: some investors, somewhere, had to be holding them.

Obvious as this seems in hindsight, a great many smart people missed it at the time. And the same thing happens every day in executive suites and board rooms as managers and company directors evaluate acquisitions, divestitures, projects, and executive compensation. As we will see, the four cornerstones of finance provide a perennially stable frame of reference for managerial decisions like these.

Mergers and acquisitions

Acquisitions are both an important source of growth for companies and an important element of a dynamic economy. Acquisitions that put companies in the hands of better owners or managers or that reduce excess capacity typically create substantial value both for the economy as a whole and for investors.

You can see this effect in the increased combined cash flows of the many companies involved in acquisitions. But although they create value overall, the distribution of that value tends to be lopsided, accruing primarily to the selling companies' shareholders. In fact, most empirical research shows that just half of the acquiring companies create value for their own shareholders.

The conservation-of-value principle is an excellent reality check for executives who want to make sure their acquisitions create value for their shareholders. The principle reminds us that acquisitions create value when the cash flows of the combined companies are greater than they would otherwise have been. Some of that value will accrue to the acquirer's shareholders if it doesn't pay too much for the acquisition.

Example of how this process works. Company A buys Company B for $1.3 billion a transaction that includes a 30 percent premium over its market value. Company A expects to increase the value of Company B by 40 percent through various operating improvements, so the value of Company B to Company A is $1.4 billion. Subtracting the purchase price of $1.3 billion from $1.4 billion leaves $100 million of value creation for Company A's shareholders.

To create value, an acquirer must achieve performance improvements that are greater than the premium paid. In other words, when the stand-alone value of the target equals the market value, the acquirer creates value for its shareholders only when the value of improvements is greater than the premium paid. With this in mind, it's easy to see why most of the value creation from acquisitions goes to the sellers' shareholders; if a company pays a 30 percent premium, it must increase the target's value by at least 30 percent to create any value.

It's worth noting that we have not mentioned an acquisition's effect on earnings per share (EPS). Although this metric is often considered, no empirical link shows that expected EPS accretion or dilution is an important indicator of whether an acquisition will create or destroy value. Deals that strengthen near-term EPS and deals that dilute near-term EPS are equally likely to create or destroy value. Bankers and other finance professionals know all this, but as one told us recently, many nonetheless "use it as a simple way to communicate with boards of directors." To avoid confusion during such communications, executives should remind themselves and their colleagues that EPS has nothing to say about which company is the best owner of specific corporate assets or about how merging two entities will change the cash flows they generate.

Divestitures

Executives are often concerned that divestitures will look like an admission of failure, make their company smaller, and reduce its stock market value. Yet the research shows that, on the contrary, the stock market consistently reacts positively to divestiture announcements. The divested business units also benefit. Research has shown that the profit margins of spun-off businesses tend to increase by one-third during the three years after the transactions are complete.

These findings illustrate the benefit of continually applying the best-owner principle: the attractiveness of a business and its best owner will probably change over time. At different stages of an industry's or company's lifespan, resource decisions that once made economic sense can become problematic. For instance, the company that invented a groundbreaking innovation may not be best suited to exploit it. Similarly, as demand falls off in a mature industry, companies that have been in it a long time are likely to have excess capacity and therefore may no longer be the best owners.

A value-creating approach to divestitures can lead to the pruning of good and bad businesses at any stage of their life cycles. Clearly, divesting a good business is often not an intuitive choice and may be difficult for managers, even if that business would be better owned by another company. It therefore makes sense to enforce some discipline in active portfolio management. One way to do so is to hold regular review meetings specifically devoted to business exits, ensuring that the topic remains on the executive agenda and that each unit receives a date stamp, or estimated time of exit.

This practice has the advantage of obliging executives to evaluate all businesses as the "sell-by date" approaches.

Executives and boards often worry that divestitures will reduce their company's size and thus cut its value in the capital markets. There follows a misconception that the markets value larger companies more than smaller ones. But this notion holds only for very small firms, with some evidence that companies with a market capitalization of less than $500 million might have slightly higher costs of capital.

Finally, executives shouldn't worry that a divestiture will dilute EPS multiples. A company selling a business with a lower P/E ratio than that of its remaining businesses will see an overall reduction in earnings per share. But don't forget that a divested underperforming unit's lower growth and ROIC potential would have previously depressed the entire company's P/E. With this unit gone, the company that remains will have a higher growth and ROIC potential and will be valued at a correspondingly higher P/E ratio. As the core-of-value principle would predict, financial mechanics, on their own, do not create or destroy value. By the way, the math works out regardless of whether the proceeds from a sale are used to pay down debt or to repurchase shares. What matters for value is the business logic of the divestiture.

Project analysis and downside risks

Reviewing the financial attractiveness of project proposals is a common task for senior executives. The sophisticated tools used to support those discounted cash flows, scenario analyses often lull top management into a false sense of security. For example, one company we know analyzed projects by using advanced statistical techniques that always showed a zero probability of a project with negative net present value (NPV). The organization did not have the ability to discuss failure, only varying degrees of success.

Such an approach ignores the core-of-value principle's laserlike focus on the future cash flows underlying returns on capital and growth, not just for a project but for the enterprise as a whole. Actively considering downside risks to future cash flows for both is a crucial subtlety of project analysis and one that often isn't undertaken.

For a moment, put yourself in the mind of an executive deciding whether to undertake a project with an upside of $80 million, a downside of −$20 million, and an expected value of $60 million. Generally accepted finance theory says that companies should take on all projects with a positive expected value, regardless of the upside-versus-downside risk.

But what if the downside would bankrupt the company? That might be the case for an electric-power utility considering the construction of a nuclear facility for $15 billion (a rough 2009 estimate for a facility with two reactors). Suppose there is an 80 percent chance the plant will be successfully constructed, brought in on time, and worth, net of investment costs, $13 billion. Suppose further that there is also a 20 percent chance that the utility company will fail to receive regulatory approval to start operating the new facility, which will then be worth − $15 billion. That means the net expected value of the facility is more than $17 billion seemingly an attractive investment.

The decision gets more complicated if the cash flow from the company's existing plants will be insufficient to cover its existing debt plus the debt on the new plant if it fails. The economics of the nuclear plant will then spill over into the value of the rest of the company which has $25 billion in existing debt and $25 billion in equity market capitalization. Failure will wipe out all the company's equity, not just the $15 billion invested in the plant. As this example makes clear, we can extend the core-of-value principle to say that a company should not take on a risk that will put its future cash flows in danger. In other words, don't do anything that has large negative spillover effects on the rest of the company. This caveat should be enough to guide managers in the earlier example of a project with an $80 million upside, a –$20 million downside, and a $60 million expected value. If a $20 million loss would endanger the company as a whole, the managers should forgo the project. On the other hand, if the project doesn't endanger the company, they should be willing to risk the $20 million loss for a far greater potential gain.

Executive compensation

This is a very hot and controversial topic however we could not conclude this chapter without talk about executive compensation! Establishing performance-based compensation systems is a daunting task, both for board directors concerned with CEO and the senior team and for human-resource leaders and other executives focused on, say, the top 500 managers. Although an entire industry has grown up around the compensation of executives, many companies continue to reward them for short-term total returns to shareholders (TRS). TRS, however, is driven more by movements in a company's industry and in the broader market (or by stock market expectations) than by individual performance. For example, many executives who became wealthy from stock options during the 1980s and 1990s saw these gains wiped out in 2008. Yet the underlying causes of share price changes such as falling interest rates in the earlier period and the financial crisis more recently were frequently disconnected from anything managers did or didn't do.

Using TRS as the basis of executive compensation reflects a fundamental misunderstanding of the third cornerstone of finance, the expectations treadmill. If investors have low expectations for a company at the beginning of a period of stock market growth, it may be relatively easy for the company's managers to beat them. But that also increases the expectations of new shareholders, so the company has to improve ever faster just to keep up and maintain its new stock price. At some point, it becomes difficult if not impossible for managers to deliver on these accelerating expectations without faltering, much as anyone would eventually stumble on a treadmill that kept getting faster.

This dynamic underscores why it's difficult to use TRS as a performance-measurement tool; extraordinary managers may deliver only ordinary TRS because it is extremely difficult to keep beating ever-higher share price expectations. Conversely, if markets have low performance expectations for a company, its managers might find it easy to earn a high TRS, at least for a short time, by raising market expectations up to the level for its peers.

Instead, compensation programs should focus on growth, returns on capital, and TRS performance, relative to peers (an important point) rather than an absolute target. That approach would eliminate much of the TRS that is not driven by company-specific performance. Such a solution sounds simple but, until recently, was made impractical by accounting rules and, in some countries, tax policies. Prior to 2004, for example, companies using US generally accepted accounting principles (GAAP) could avoid listing stock options as an

113

expense on their income statements provided they met certain criteria, one of which was that the exercise price had to be fixed. To avoid taking an earnings hit, companies avoided compensation systems based on relative performance, which would have required more flexibility in structuring options.

Since 2004, a few companies have moved to share-based compensation systems tied to relative performance. GE, for one, granted its CEO a performance award based on the company's TRS relative to the TRS of the S&P 500 index. We hope that more companies will follow this direction.

Applying the four cornerstones of finance sometimes means going against the crowd. It means accepting that there are no free lunches. It means relying on data, thoughtful analysis, and a deep understanding of the competitive dynamics of an industry. None of this is easy, but the payoff, the creation of value for a company's stakeholders and for society at large is enormous.

Chapter 16: CEO's Guide to Social Media

CEOs who shun social media risk losing touch with some of their most lucrative customers, prospects and influencers. A study released recently found that 76% of executives want their CEOs to be active on social media, while another study found that only 5.6% of Fortune 500 CEOs are active on Twitter. What's all this adds up to? A massive guilt trip for anti-social CEOs.

Guilt leads to one of two choices; 1) action, or 2) rationalization. There are some who say most CEOs shouldn't be on Twitter. I agree. But some should be, and if you are one of those that should be then don't use such opinions to rationalize making a poor decision. Take action instead. Here are 3 high-level tips for getting started, followed by more detailed, specific advice.

1.   Do It. If you are merely going to set up social media profiles and then do nothing with them, that is another reason to avoid social media altogether. Warren Buffett first tweeted on May 2nd, 2013. He has tweeted a grand total of three times since then. He is also not following a single other Twitter user. When he had no profile his admirers could justify it. But to set up a profile and then not use it makes it look as though Buffett is asleep at the wheel. It's worse than if he had never set up a profile in the first place. Look to Richard Branson as an example to follow. He follows over 4,020 other Twitter users, and has tweeted over 5,118 times as of the time writing this book. He follows his own advice to corporate leaders regarding social media, "Be authentic and

organic. It can't be forced or it won't work. And most importantly, have fun."

2.   Do It Yourself. If you are not going to control your own social media profiles, then you shouldn't be on social media. Being social does not mean tasking your marketing department with setting up social media profiles with your name on them and posting content as if they were you. If you are going to do this then you might as well just set up a corporate profile or direct people to the "press" section of your website. Being effective on social media means being authentic, and that means the content being posted needs to come directly from you. If it doesn't, it will be obvious to your followers and you will get little to no traction, even if you are a business superstar who can attract lots of followers by dint of your name alone.

3.   Do It Now. I know what you are thinking. "This sounds interesting; I will have to look into this next week." You and I both know that is code for "I don't want to admit to myself that I am scared to do this, afraid I will look like an idiot, and so I am going to use the excuse of being too busy and put it off indefinitely, hopefully forever." Look at this as an opportunity, not an obligation.

Why Future CEOs Must Quietly Embrace Social Media

If you are a CEO who doesn't tweet, you are obviously not alone. You are in the vast majority. If you are comfortable following the crowd, then there's no reason to keep reading this chapter. But if, like me a few months ago, you've become uneasy about your lack of acumen when it comes to social media, I have created a simple guide to getting started with social media, from one CEO to another. Note that this is not a definitive guide on how CEOs can become social media experts. This is how you dip your toes in and get started.

LinkedIn

The easiest social network for CEOs to use and appreciate. Get started here by creating a full profile, connecting with those you know, and joining groups that are interesting to you. At least once a week post something to the LinkedIn homepage. It can be an article (along with your brief comments on it) or just your thoughts by themselves. Ask questions. Invite feedback.

Twitter

After LinkedIn I would focus on Twitter. I found it difficult to get started on Twitter, but easier to use once I got used to it. Don't want to look stupid asking for advice? Check out Michael Hyatt's Beginner's Guide to Twitter. Once you have set up your account create a schedule for tweeting by inserting a reminder in your calendar. Tweet once a day. It's only 140 characters; it won't take much of your time. Retweet interesting posts from people you follow. And by the way, follow a lot of people anyone whose opinion you respect. Commit to using Twitter at least once a day for a month. I resisted Twitter for years, but one week of being committed to using it was all it took to make me an addict.

Facebook

As a CEO, think of Facebook as a bit of LinkedIn and Twitter combined. Sure, there is more to it than that, but that is enough to get you started.

117

Google+

"Ah, geez, do I have to?" Yes. Google+ is sneaking up on Facebook, and as a recent convert to Google+ I believe him. It's not quite there yet, in my opinion, and it lacks the active network Facebook has, but I wouldn't be surprised if Google+ ends up being a Facebook-killer.

Pinterest

I will confess, I am not very active on Pinterest…yet. It's on my to-do list. I have dabbled with it, but more for personal reasons than for business. If that is all you have time to do, at least get started that way. Then start reading resources on doing business on Pinterest. One of the biggest mistakes marketers make is that they don't create enough original content. This is an area where you can enlist the help of your marketing team. Have them create content for you, then you post it with your authentic comments. Or share visuals related to the operations of your business. Did you just set up a new office? Pin pictures of it. New product? A photo of every product you sell should be posted to Pinterest with a link to where it can be purchased.

Instagram

Don't use Instagram the way you might use Pinterest. We would advise businesses to start out listening with Instagram, rather than talking. That is sound advice. By the way, you need to be using a mobile device to sign up, unless you want to get fancy.

Goodreads

I am a firm believer in the Charlie Jones quote "Five years from today, you will be the same person that you are today, except for the books you read and the people you meet." I am nose down in anywhere from 5 to 10 books at any given time, and anyone who knows me knows I love to talk about books, recommend books, and give books as gifts. Goodreads is a social network custom made for bookophiles like me, and it allows me to connect with business associates, employees, and clients on a very personal level. Just set up an account, connect with your Facebook friends, and start adding books you have read.

I could talk about Reddit, StumbleUpon, and another 50 social media websites, but I consider the above to be the basic ones any CEO new to social media should start with.

Chapter 17: CEO Guide to Board Composition

In this chapter we will review the numerous factors affecting the composition of European supervisory boards and offers a model of director attributes to guide boards in refining their composition strategy.

European supervisory boards are significantly rethinking how best to fulfil their responsibilities in a time of economic turbulence, changing markets and accelerating globalisation. A good part of the discussion focuses on the issue of supervisory board composition and the qualities to be sought in individual directors and on the board as a whole.

You want to be able to look around the boardroom table and see the different stakeholders represented so that when an issue comes up that involves one of them, you have an experienced person to turn to on that matter.

Historically, boards were often very homogeneous institutions, composed largely of men from the same country. Relevant industry expertise frequently was seen as less important than a reputation for collegiality. Extended tenure and extensive board interlocks were not uncommon. Today, the situation is in flux, with European boards displaying a great deal of variation on the questions of gender, nationality and professional background. Shareholders, regulators and boards themselves are questioning the assumptions that have shaped board composition; there is no one view of what the ideal board should look like. Instead, nominating committees have to balance a number of opposing considerations.

Continuity vs. Fresh perspective

Against the background of the global economic downturn, there is a desire to recruit directors with fresh perspectives as well as experience and competencies suited to the challenges at hand. In addition, there is growing appreciation of the fact that boards composed of members with varying perspectives are more likely to ask the important questions rather than succumbing to "group think". At the same time, however, boards want to preserve and leverage their existing institutional knowledge and relationships.

Cohesion vs. Diversity

Because of their collaborative nature, supervisory boards, particularly at older companies, often have placed a premium on selecting directors who fit easily into the existing boardroom culture. As a result, CEOs, chairmen and nominating committees frequently turned toward their own professional and social networks when looking for director candidates, reinforcing boardroom homogeneity. Increasingly, however, there is recognition that boards composed entirely of men from the company's home country are at a disadvantage in a world of two genders and of global markets and supply chains. The issue for boards is to incorporate diverse perspectives while maintaining the cohesion and trust that are essential for the board to function properly.

Granular expertise vs. big-picture oversight

Historically, supervisory boards have placed less emphasis on directors having industry-specific competencies. After all, it was the job of the executive board to manage the enterprise; the supervisory board's mission was to provide the oversight that comes from experienced, but more general, business judgement.

Oversight is still the supervisory board's responsibility. But the complexities of today's business issues increasingly demand that supervisory directors have the appropriate expertise to engage their executive counterparts in substantive discussion and provide meaningful counsel to CEO.

Corporate governance vs. Corporate growth

The events leading up to the current economic crisis have led to calls for supervisory boards to take a more proactive role in risk mitigation. This need is undeniable (and is a continuation of similar measures taken in the wake of the Enron scandal). At the same time, however, there is a growing sentiment that supervisory boards need to plan beyond the current environment and devote substantial focus to ensuring that the executive board is maximising value creation. This requires directors who themselves have extensive track records in driving corporate growth.

Balancing each of these considerations is not a question of "either/or" but "both". The challenge for each nominating committee is finding the right proportion of the various attributes to be represented and translating that into a strategy that drives its board member appointments.

A New Model of Director Attributes

The number of qualities to be considered when managing board composition complicates the identification of director candidates. To help boards in this process, we developed a multidimensional model that outlines the range of attributes that interact with each other to form a director's overall perspective:

- Experiential attributes, such as education, industry experience, functional experience and accomplishments.
- Demographic attributes, including gender, ethnicity, geography and generation.
- Personal attributes, including personality, cultural adaptability, interests and values.

These attributes combine to influence the perspectives that people draw upon and the lens through which they approach the world. These perspectives, in turn, shape these competencies an executive develops, the priorities that guide his or her work, and the insights that he or she generates in solving problems, identifying opportunities and assessing risks.

This multidimensional model provides a starting point that allows nominating committees to more consciously shape and optimise the collective skills and dynamics of the board by identifying the full range of variables to be considered. Analysis of these variables should be included in the candidate assessment process through interviews, referencing, psychometric analyses and other techniques.

Assessing the Current Situation

While each board handles composition in its own way, it is possible to look at certain variables in the aggregate to get a sharper picture of how change is unfolding at the largest publicly traded companies in each country.

Gender: Gender has been the most vocal component in the discussion over diversity in board composition. Across Europe, companies have responded in very different ways. Thirty-nine percent of the directors of Norway's largest companies are now women, following recent legislation there requiring each gender to have at least 40 percent representation on the boards of most large companies. Many other countries, however, such as France, Germany and Spain are in the 5 percent to 10 percent range. Historically, companies have responded to the issue of gender imbalance by pointing to a lack of women executives with C-level experience from which to draw. Here, Norway's example is instructive. Forced by legislation to recruit women to their boards, Norwegian companies cast a wider net, recruiting from the pool of women just below the traditional top tier and also looking beyond Norway itself, thus increasing international representation. Casting a wider net, however, has placed an even greater emphasis on the rigorous and objective evaluation of the prospective director's capabilities to ensure that he or she will be able to contribute at the required level, particularly when it comes to the central board responsibility of evaluating management. There is significant debate within the European business community regarding whether or not some women executives in Norway have found themselves in a board member's seat prematurely, doing a disservice to both the individual and the company.

Nationality: While barriers to globalised markets have fallen dramatically over the last 20 years, boards have been slower to draw their directors from outside the company's home country. There are several reasons for this. To begin with, in many countries, there has been a sense that its flagship enterprises are part of the country's cultural patrimony, something that is reflected in a board composed of the business leaders of that country. But that attitude is softening in the face of globalisation. For example, the boards of Denmark's largest companies, which a few years ago had little foreign representation, now have foreign representation of nearly 25 percent.

At the same time, however, linguistic and logistical barriers remain. Globalising the board usually means conducting board businesses in a second language, something with which all directors may not be comfortable, particularly on boards with significant employee representation. More important, while directors from the Americas or Asia may be able to attend regularly scheduled board meetings, they might find it difficult to fully participate in the ad hoc events and gatherings that inevitably occur. A board thus risks dividing itself into "inner" and "outer" subgroups not a recipe for building a cohesive board.

Age and Tenure: The national averages of director age are remarkably consistent from country to country, with the majority falling between 57 and 62 years.

More telling, however, is the percentage of directors who have served on their boards for more than nine years, the outer limit of what is recommended by the United Kingdom's Combined Code of Corporate Governance in the interest of a "planned and progressive refreshing of the board." In a significant number of countries, roughly one-quarter of board members are past this benchmark, suggesting that the issue of boardroom succession planning still requires closer examination.

Industry Experience: Until fairly recently, nominating committees tended to place the greatest priority on recruiting board members with successful CEO experience, irrespective of the industry from which they came. Today, however, there is an increased premium placed on have industry-specific experience in the boardroom, as supervisory and executive boards look to engage each other in more substantial discussions regarding business issues. This does not necessarily mean, however, that the supervisory board should replicate the technical competencies found on the executive team. As well as appointing board members from the same industry, a potential strategy is to add executives from adjacent industries. A retailer might add a board member from the consumer packaged goods sector; a telecommunications company might look for a director from retail, providing a range of relevant perspectives from which the board can engage management on issues of strategy and operations.

Implications for Boards

Aligning a board's composition with the challenges and opportunities it faces in a rapidly changing, globalised world and then building that group into a cohesive unit requires a sustained effort by the board, its nominating committee and its chair. The following practices are particularly critical

Nominating committees must approach board composition strategically. Beginning with the direction of the company and the issues it is facing (both now and five years from now); nominating committees must identify the attributes needed to address those issues in the boardroom. Next, the committee must assess the current board and its attributes against what is required to identify gaps to be addressed. This analysis should include the industry and functional competencies of the board and should evaluate whether or not they are adequate to fully engage the management team.

Use rigorous candidate search and evaluation process. Guided by the above requirements, boards must continue to move beyond personal, tight-knit networks when looking for directors. A rigorous candidate interview and evaluation process focusing on core competencies is essential to ensure that while directors may have different perspectives and backgrounds, they share the ability to perform at the level required. In addition to the competencies dictated by the board's specific needs, the nominating committee must screen for competencies needed to succeed in a diverse environment, such as cultural astuteness and communication skills.

Place greater emphasis on the board's process and role of the chairman. Having a more diverse board means expending extra effort to build the group into a cohesive unit. The responsibility for doing so rests with the board chair and the choices he or she makes regarding committee assignments, board policies and board culture. A well-thought out onboarding program, as well as ongoing, detailed education regarding company operations is critical. Details such as how many site visits a board should conduct each year and how often the board gathers for dinners and other opportunities for social interaction take on greater importance with a more diverse board.

Make board assessment a priority. Board processes should include a rigorous, annual assessment of both the collective board and individual directors. Forward-thinking boards have external consultants conduct the assessments every three years to ensure objectivity and the use of best practices. Such assessment creates the shared standards and expectations that transform the board into a high-performing organisation.

Board composition will continue to be a defining issue for European companies as they look to engage with their management teams on a more substantial level, reflect the perspectives and concerns of their global shareholders and stakeholders, and act as a strategic resource in a time of permeable geographic borders and disappearing industry silos. Boards and nominating committees must assess in an ongoing, systematic process the mix of attributes needed around the boardroom table, and the board chair must create a platform of trust, cohesion and common standards. This effort will pay off by allowing the board to be a truly strategic resource for the various stakeholders, CEO and senior management team during a time of rapid change.

Chapter 18: Why Diversity Matters in the Boardroom

Way back when, it all made sense. Having people on your board of directors who were reliable, like-minded and known entities was the most logical strategy to build a board. After all, the purpose of the board was to support the chief executive officer's (CEO) plan and assure the shareholders that experienced, intelligent people were looking out for their interests.

Even if this strategy was well-intentioned, it came with a number of significant downsides. First, it created an environment in which directors were beholden to CEO for their seat; something that clearly undermined board independence. Second, a board built on a handful of relationships has the inherent risk of insularity. This homogeneity can be a hindrance in an increasingly dynamic environment. As globalization, the rapid deployment of technology, an increasing need for risk management and the shifting demographics of workforces made businesses much more complex, boards began to broaden their composition. But diversity for its own sake falls short of both the need and the opportunity. An evolution is under way, and boards now are beginning to realize that it is the breadth of perspective, not the mere inclusion of various diverse traits, that benefits the organization.

Constructing a quality board is about the calibre and perspective of individual directors chosen as well as the deliberate creation of a dynamic and a chemistry that allow for the effective execution of corporate governance and strategic oversight. The board's primary responsibilities can vary, yet typically include identifying and evaluating significant opportunities and risks, serving as informed counsel for major strategic decisions and assessing CEO's performance. Executing these changes requires two general conditions:

1. Individuals who are experienced, responsible and collaborative.
2. An environment in which challenging issues can be confronted, opposing opinions are sought and trust is implicit.

This complicates the task of the board nominating committee, which has taken the lead in shaping the composition of the board. How does the board determine the characteristics sought in new directors and the combination of them whose service will be in the best interest of the company? Which candidates should be selected, especially in the context of those already on the board? What guideposts should nominating committees use given the wide latitude public companies have in who they place on their boards?

In view of the evolving responsibilities and influences of boards, we set about to study how boardroom heterogeneity is perceived and valued by directors. Our focus was gender, as there has been a significant amount of change regarding women in the boardroom over the last decade. We were less interested in the often-quoted statistics and "glass ceiling" issues that have been analyzed and discussed by many before us and instead set out to go further, to identify why it is important to have a diversity of perspective in the boardroom. As we began to probe, we realized that our findings on this issue transcend gender to address a broader subject. How does diversity of perspective in the boardroom lead to a good dynamic and better governance? How can boards better structure themselves to benefit their constituents? Finally, how can candidates and nominating committees respond to the opportunities and needs that already exist?

Our Learnings

Our conversations with women and men directors from a wide range of Fortune 250 companies focused on two central topics:
1. The way in which directors view having a diverse perspective
2. The degree to which directorships are accessible to a diverse pool of candidates.

We learned that:
- A wide range of perspectives, not merely token representation, is critical to effective corporate governance.
- The trend toward diversity is essential as boards look to navigate the complex and dynamic issues that companies now face.
- Boards become greater advocates for diversity as they have more direct beneficial experiences with it.
- It is incumbent upon board members and the candidates themselves to reach out to each other at a time when the adage of "who you know" is being replaced by "how you know them."

What the Statistics Told Us

We found it a useful starting point to look into the composition of Fortune 250 companies' boards of directors. We learned the following:

Fortune 250 boards include a large number of women directors from non-business sectors. Women from government service, academia, nonprofits and the legal profession currently account for nearly half of all women directors. Among women directors who have joined these boards more recently, however, we see an increase in those with corporate backgrounds. This trend is not surprising. A decade and more ago, women with significant professional accomplishment were more likely to be found in universities, foundations and government, sectors that were quicker to lower the barriers to their most senior leadership ranks. As more women gain C-suite experience, director candidate pools are bolstered.

There are telling differences among sectors in the distribution of women directors. At first glance, the industrial sector appears to be a leader in the inclusion of women in the boardroom. Every industrial company in the Fortune 250 has at least one woman on its board; this cannot be claimed by any other sector. However, companies in the industrial sector more often have only one woman on their board, and, as a result, industrial companies have the lowest average number of women on their board. Companies with a critical mass of women on their board (three or more) are more likely to be in the financial services sector, with consumer products, healthcare/pharmaceuticals and technology/ telecom a step behind. It is surprising, nonetheless, that not one of these sectors can claim that 100 percent of their companies have at least one woman on their board.

The board committees on which directors sit often reflect numerous factors. We found that women are most likely to serve on nominating/governance committees and are least often seen on executive committees. Our anecdotal findings

134

suggest that women are perceived as being particularly valuable on nominating committees because these directors represent a desired diversity group (the old reason), and they bring a broader perspective (the new reason). Notably, women are underrepresented among the ranks of those chairing committees. This, along with the underrepresentation on executive committees, may be a function of the influence that board tenure plays in determining these roles. Other factors could be at work here as well.

What We Heard from Directors

The directors with whom we spoke were passionate about the topic of diversity of perspective, both in general and in the specific case of gender. They had strong opinions about the effect of bringing different perspectives to the boardroom, the qualities most sought in directors and the paths that lead to the boardroom.

Here is what we heard:

Having a wide range of perspectives represented in the boardroom is critical to effective corporate governance.

Having multiple views on the possible outcomes of any action makes for a decision-making process that is more likely to take into account the various risks, consequences and implications of possible actions. "Increasingly, boards are in a fishbowl of scrutiny from investors, the media, non-governmental organizations and so on. The problems that boards are grappling with are too hard for any one person to figure out," one director told us. Another director observed that, "You want directors to have experience in dealing with risk from many angles because you don't know where your risk is going to come from. Having directors from very diverse backgrounds really helps."

A board needs to take into consideration all of its constituencies. While no one disputes that a board's first responsibility is to the company's shareholders, those shareholders suffer without the support of customers and employees. A diverse board allows for the group to better anticipate and consider the concerns and perspectives of all key constituencies.

Being able to draw upon a diverse set of competencies and knowledge is essential if boards are to successfully address the complex issues their companies face.

A board needs to draw upon a range of experiences in understanding opportunities, anticipating challenges and assessing risks. Rarely does a right or wrong answer exist for the many issues a board faces, particularly in an environment where silos defining industries are breaking down, constituencies are globalizing, the effects of technology are accelerating and risk presents itself in new ways. With these lines blurring, having multiple views on the possible outcomes of an action results in a more thoughtful decision-making process.

A board needs to constantly challenge itself to keep pace with the changing dynamics a company faces. This is best done through a robust dialogue of differing views as long as they are offered respectfully and listened to carefully. "People tend to get insular, and it's incredibly important for boards to get different perspectives," said one director. "That there is not one right answer is not as easily grasped as one might think."

Boards become more appreciative of having a broad perspective as they accumulate experience in dealing with it.

The directors with whom we spoke saw the benefits of diversity as having been established beyond dispute. "Diversity and inclusion are not just the right thing to do but are important to the business agenda," said one director. "Boards are at their best when there is diversity of culture, thinking and perspective."

All directors reported that constructively challenging the status quo is healthy. As one woman director with more than two decades of board service recounted, "I helped people move from the notion of 'Being different is bad,' to 'Being different is good.' In other words, diversity is not deviant."

While many of the women directors reported that gender played at least some role in their earliest directorship nominations, these women didn't consider it an ongoing factor. Once they garnered the experience and reputation for effectiveness as a board member, the calls came because of individual capabilities and perspective, not because these candidates simply represented a targeted demographic. As one reported, "Being a woman was instrumental to my first board. After that, it was reputation as a good board member."

Strategies to influence gender diversity still are evolving

The adage of "who you know" is being replaced with "how you know them." As with most men, the majority of women directors reached their first board seat because someone actively championed them. Whether recommended by a CEO for whom they worked or a board member who saw them in action, new initiates to the boardroom often are introduced by more experienced directors who can vouch for them. It isn't, then, a question of being known by the right people but rather having an opportunity to impress them and be mentored by them. Said one director, "An inexperienced board candidate needs interaction with other board members and CEOs to create comfort among those who are in a position of influence."

Women are increasingly making their way into the boardroom, in part because of the greater number of women in the C-suite who make up the pool of eligible candidates. As important, heightened awareness during the past decade of the pitfalls of homogeneity has contributed to more women in the boardroom. We see a trend, its sustainability unknown, that boards are increasingly focusing their recruiting efforts on directors who bring a diverse perspective to the challenging requirements of governance and improved board performance rather than those who are selected because of demographic traits.

It would be a mistake, however, to conclude that women face no obstacles to reaching the boardroom. Some of the directors with whom we spoke told us that women still occasionally encounter outdated stereotyping on the path to earning credibility and respect. In fairness, one director referred to this as "a conditioned response for the older generation," and our findings confirm that these attitudes are becoming increasingly rare.

We would be remiss not to mention that there also were many robust discussions about what characterizes the behavioural differences between women and men. We will stop short of opening that can of worms so that we stay on point with our message. Having differences is a good thing, and celebrating them is even better. Suffice it to say, the behavioural differences between the genders constitute a science unto itself.

A New Model of Director Competencies and Perspectives

"Anyone who can only think of only one way to spell a word obviously lacks imagination." Ade Asefeso.

As we noted earlier, gender is only one of many attributes that contribute to the perspective that a director brings to the boardroom. In fact traditional approaches to diversity recruiting have tended to focus on one or two specific variables at a time; we need to add a marketing person to the board, or we need to find someone who is ethnically diverse. While this has been a step in the right direction, boards would benefit from nominating committees that are charged to take a more holistic, multidimensional view. Such an approach would help them better build boards that can draw upon a wide range of perspectives, as well as experience and knowledge, as part of their candidate assessment process.

In our experience, an executive's perspective is influenced by a combination of three different sets of attributes:
1. Experiential attributes, such as functional experience, industry experience, accomplishments and education.
2. Demographic attributes, including gender, race, region and generational cohort.
3. Personal attributes, including personality, interests and values.

Our interviews confirm that this broad way of thinking about what informs leaders directly impacts how they contribute in

139

the boardroom. Further, the concomitant nature of these attributes shapes how each individual approaches a situation and responds to others with similar or varying attributes.

These attributes combine to influence the perspectives that people draw upon and the lens through which they approach the world. These perspectives, in turn, shape the competencies an executive develops, the priorities that guide his or her work, and the insights that he or she generates in solving problems, identifying opportunities and assessing risks.

This multidimensional model provides a starting point that allows nominating committees to more consciously shape and optimize the collective skills and dynamics of the board by identifying the full range of variables to be considered. Analysis of these variables should be included in the candidate assessment process, including interviews, referencing, psychometric analysis and other techniques.

A board composed of directors representing a range of perspectives leads to an environment of collaborative tension that is the essence of good governance. In a room where everyone has different points of view and there is a greater opportunity for cross-pollination of ideas, there are fewer unspoken assumptions, less "group think" and a greater likelihood of innovation. This allows the board to ask the probing questions and tackle the challenging issues, such as risk management and succession planning, which are at the centre of good corporate governance.

Implications for Nominating Committees

I not only use all the brains that I have but all that I can borrow." Ade Asefeso!

Creating a board composed of directors with a broad range of perspectives must be a conscious choice by the nominating committee. The natural tendency to turn to our own networks when looking to identify candidates can easily give rise to self-reinforcing homogeneity. Often, we are not aware of how limited our own networks are when compared with the full universe of qualified candidates.

The benefits of having a diverse board are particularly powerful when there is a critical mass of varied perspectives to support broad thinking. "A board is better off if the representation is as well-balanced as you can get it," one male director told us. The effects of critical mass were confirmed in a recent Wellesley College study focused on gender in the boardroom, which showed improved dynamics with three or more women on a board and consequent advantages in board governance.

To be clear, we do not suggest that breadth of perspective is to be diverse for its own sake. Diversity without cohesion can result in what one director refers to as a "cacophony of voices." Instead, board members must be able to draw upon a certain foundation of deep business experience and judgment and, more important, must be chosen in ways that align with the strategic needs of the company. The challenge of the nominating committee is to compose the board so that the creative tension of different perspectives and personalities exists within a coherent framework that serves the needs of the organization. As one director put it, "Good governance, by definition, is having a breadth of perspective. It is about bringing in ideas from elsewhere. A board that is not getting the quality of input it needs will likely have a loose approach to governance and a less disciplined approach to business."

There are several ways in which nominating committees can successfully incorporate breadth of perspective into their candidate selection process:

Determine the set of competencies, priorities and insights to be sought and establish a process for screening for those qualities. In addition to needed functional or regional expertise, it is critical to include other competencies, such as conceptual thinking, resilience and the ability to manage ambiguity that are prerequisites to adding value to boardroom discussions. The list, of course, will vary for each situation and requires thoughtful analysis by the nominating committee.

Conduct a gap analysis of the board that considers that full range of attributes. A gap analysis can be a helpful tool to identify the experience and competencies represented around the boardroom table and those that are lacking. Traditional gap analyses, however, usually are focused on a fairly select range of competencies and professional accomplishments, such as CEO experience or financial expertise. By expanding the analysis to include the full range of competencies sought and the experimental, demographic and personal attributes that form perspective, a nominating committee can act with greater awareness of the variables at work in shaping a board.

Place priority on effective communications kills and interpersonal acumen. Every director with whom we spoke emphasized that effective communication is essential to competent directorship. This is all the more so in a diverse environment where shared perspective cannot be assumed. Director candidates should have a track record of successfully working with multiple constituencies and building support for difficult undertakings. They should be able to succinctly and clearly express their point of view, probe and learn from the perspective of others, and extract solutions from the flow of boardroom dialogue. As one director put it, an effective director is one who can "stand out for what you bring to the table and fit in so that you can be listened to."

Cast a wider net. Our conversations suggest that there is a substantial pool of developing talent of women immediately below the C-suite level that can be tapped into if nominating committees are willing to look a little deeper. These candidates can contribute additional competencies and perspective, in addition to uncommon energy and drive. "When diversity becomes a requirement for the candidate pool, it makes for a better search," said one director. "It forces the issue of people getting comfortable with people who are not like them." As one woman director who was tapped for a directorship while still a vice president commented, "They reached down for me, and it was a gift to both of us."

Ensure a meaningful director evaluation process. A diverse board is united by common boardroom standards and goals. A thorough director evaluation process is central to maintaining that touchstone. "Boards need to get beyond the 'clubby' perspective that keeps them from providing robust direction and evaluation of their members," in the words of one boardroom veteran.

Diversity of perspective does matter. Having a broad range of collective attributes, rather than overlapping or redundant qualities, helps the board significantly in fulfilling its responsibilities of providing good corporate governance and strategic oversight. Boards that can collectively draw upon a broad assortment of competencies, priorities and insights are an invaluable resource for CEOs and senior management teams working in complex business environments with wide-ranging, multiple constituencies. Diversity of perspective leads to more innovation, better risk management, and stronger connections with customers, employees and business partners.

While tremendous progress has been made, there is significant work yet to be done. Notwithstanding many encouraging findings of our study, women often still are approached for boards because they represent a diverse demographic and not because they bring a specific, needed perspective. The good news is that the pool of C-suite women is expanding, and boards are becoming increasingly attuned in their thinking about the importance of maintaining a broad perspective. While our conversations focused on women in the boardroom, we are confident that these findings transcend the gender issue.

Chapter 19: CEO Guide to High Performing Board

As the UK Combined Code of Corporate Governance 2003 states:

"Every company should be headed by an effective board, which is collectively responsible for the success of the company."

The scrutiny placed upon public company boards continues to intensify. Stakeholders from regulators to shareholders to corporate social responsibility advocates have become more vocal, more sophisticated and less forgiving, while the business environment has become more complicated and more competitive. In particular, three forces have combined to increase the pressure on boards:

1. Shareholders: Both short-term and long-term investors are expecting boards to play a greater role in ensuring that shareholder value is maximised, and shareholders are quicker to issue challenges when they are displeased. The recent expansion of private equity to the acquisition and management of large companies has made this more acute, forcing boards to measure their own performance and decision making against that of a theoretical (or sometimes very real) private equity purchaser.

2. Global business environment: Increased globalisation, the accelerated pace of change and competition, the impact of technologies and the ever-increasing focus

145

on costs (both across the supply chain and through operational productivity) are all increasing risks and opportunities, heightening the importance of the board's oversight function. It is also placing a greater emphasis on board composition, given the value that can be added by board members with strategically critical skills and experience.

3. Chief Executive Officers (CEOs): It is no secret that boards have become more demanding of CEOs in recent years, as the declining average tenure of CEOs clearly shows. At the same time, however, CEOs are becoming more demanding of their board members particularly of their non-executive directors (NEDs), who are looked to for their independent judgment and perspective on both short-term and long-term strategic issues. CEOs are demanding that boards fulfil their governance duties efficiently, while supporting the building of the senior executive team and guiding succession planning. Indeed, we find that CEOs are often setting higher standards in this regard than their non-executive chairmen, and some are frustrated by the perceived quality of their NEDs.

Diagnostic Questions

There is no set definition of what constitutes a high-performing board; indeed, there may be too many variables for a comprehensive description. At the same time, however, there is a set of diagnostic questions that CEOs, chairmen and corporate secretaries can ask to help frame the issues.

1. What do the various stakeholders (investors, regulators, the management team, banks,

communities where the company has operations, etc.) expect from the company as an institution and from the board in its oversight role?

2. What does CEO need and expect from the board in terms of functional expertise, senior team building and succession planning, strategic guidance, etc.?

3. How do the chairman and CEO define quality participation and contribution? Are those expectations clearly communicated through an effective induction process and measured through a regular individual and collective board evaluation process?

4. Are the board's policies and practices as rigorous and effective as they should be? Beyond the mere meeting of regulatory requirements, does the board use its experience and expertise to help drive company performance?

5. How does the Nominations Committee assess the competencies and skills needed for the board given the company's particular opportunities and challenges, and how does it identify potential board members in a way that goes beyond the "usual suspects"?

6. Are there well-defined boundaries between the board and the executive team so that oversight does not encroach upon operations?

7. Does the board have the strength and depth to steer the company through a financial crisis, a reputation-damaging event or sudden CEO resignation?

Elements of High Performance

While each company will answer these questions differently, our experience in working with boards suggests that high-performing boards focus on a common set of tasks, which include the following:

1. Responding to executive strategy and contributing to rigorous debate. (The board brings fresh perspectives; it does not originate strategy.)
2. Monitoring the implementation of the strategy through the operational plans.
3. Overseeing the quality of leadership and management, ensuring that individuals are developed and that effective succession plans are in place.
4. Maintaining a governance framework that adds value to the business.
5. Safeguarding the company's values and reputation.

Characteristics of the High-Performing Board

What do boards need to be able to successfully accomplish these tasks and meet the expectations of their various stakeholders? We find that the best boards have four common characteristics:

1. Clarity regarding role and focus: High-performing boards begin with a clear understanding of their role, scope of responsibilities and expected contribution to the long-term success of the company. Some boards have a formal charter that covers these points and which can serve as a touchstone to ensure continuity and common understanding.

2. An effective chairman: The chairman sets the board's tone and direction as well as its performance culture. He or she creates the appropriate environment for full engagement by all members of the board, drawing out opinions and shaping discussions of sensitive issues. Beyond the board and committee meetings,

the most effective chairmen spend time with their NEDs individually as frequently as once a quarter to ensure that issues are discussed, performance is assessed, and timely and effective contributions are encouraged. The chairman manages the process of integrating NEDs and executives into a cohesive team in which all parties are aware of their responsibilities and boundaries. Finally, effective chairmen have established an open and honest relationship with their CEO based on mutual trust and understanding.

3. A balanced board team: A board is only as good as its members particularly the NEDs, who bring the outside perspective and judgment on which the board's oversight function is predicated. And like many things in business, recruiting the right NEDs is something that is easy to talk about but hard to execute. A high-performing board includes NEDs who can provide broad strategic perspective while also bringing their specific experience and expertise to bear on boardroom issues ranging from the environment and climate change to globalisation. And high-performing boards are balanced not just with respect to expertise but to temperament as well, mixing analytical thinkers with visionaries, conciliators with challengers. Once the team is built, the chairmen of high-performing boards spend considerable effort integrating their NEDs and executive members; holding committee meetings the day before the board meeting, blending social interaction with substantive discussion at board dinners and, as ever, encouraging participation. Indeed, the conversation between CEO and the board should be fluid and ongoing. CEO needs to be comfortable with using the group as a

sounding board for ideas in their formative stage, so that he or she can get the full benefit of the board's expertise.

4. A culture of trust and respect: A board is not a collection of individuals and talents but a team. For it to function as such, effective chemistry, candid communication and mutual respect are critical. This ensures that probing questioning, constructive criticism and challenging debate can take place between the NEDs and the executive team. It is through what one chairman calls "the bit of thrust", that the company truly reaps the benefits of an engaged board.

Quality Control Through Practices and Processes

In the past, many companies relied on the chairman's force of personality to determine and enforce the board's standards and practices. The increasing scrutiny of board performance, however, is placing an emphasis on the establishment of certain key processes that provide a framework for consistency and excellence. These processes include the following:

1. An agenda: A transparent rolling board agenda that includes financial, strategic, governance, operational and human capital issues provides the structural framework for the board's oversight. Agendas should be flexible enough to recognise that issues evolve in real time rather than neatly fitting the board's calendar and should allow for board members to bring forth unscheduled topics. A good chairman is also continually assessing the board's preparedness for the

unexpected, introducing discussion of hypothetical scenarios (a hostile takeover, a financial markets crisis and so on) at appropriate points. The board agenda should both inform and be aligned with the Executive Committee agenda and should be accompanied by the appropriate documentation and data to allow for informed discussion.

2. An annual calendar: This document ensures that certain big-picture items, including long-term planning, strategy, operational plans and performance, succession planning, crisis management and human capital, are discussed by the board on a regular basis.

3. Communications and reporting: The responsibilities of board committees and their reporting processes must be clear and supported by effective communications among the board, the company secretary and the Executive Committee.

4. Structured engagement: In order for non-executive directors to make informed contributions, they need to get out of the boardroom and into the business, spending time with executives below the board level. Forward-thinking chairmen have NEDs accompany senior and middle management to meetings and conferences and link together NED management pairs on regular tours out in the field. Asking NEDs to give a short report at each board meeting regarding their engagement activities and learning adds an effective element of accountability and peer pressure to the process.

5. Performance measurement and management: Measuring individual and collective performance is critical. Individual measurement begins with a formal induction and is sustained through regular appraisal processes. The performance of individuals and the board as a team should be validated by benchmarking and verified by independent external specialists.

There is no one recipe for having a high-performing board. Our observations suggest, however, that it requires a combination of "hard" components (including robust structures, clear roles and responsibilities, and rigorous processes and administration) and "soft" components (including directors with the right competencies to address the company's short-term and long-term issues and a strong chairman who has a healthy relationship with CEO and who can establish a culture of vigorous discussion and effective decision making for the entire board).

Both areas require continuous focus and commitment to improve, particularly from the chairman, to ensure that the board's performance bar is raised. In reality, however, too few boards address both components with the necessary sustained rigour. Many either fail to identify and address areas for improvement or fail to commit the energy and resources necessary for real growth. We suspect that some chairmen may still be caught in a comfort zone, insulating themselves from either internal or external pressure to change.

In the current competitive environment, however, those pressures will continue to build more and more boards are responding by taking a close look at their performance in order to avoid undermining investor confidence, inviting regulatory scrutiny or depriving management of the benefits of quality oversight.

Companies are finding that a formal third-party board assessment and performance benchmarking exercise can provide a helpful first step in moving chairmen and boards outside of their comfort zones and in identifying opportunities for strengthening corporate governance and overall board performance.

We will continue to investigate these corporate governance and board performance issues and share our findings. In so doing, we aim to prompt discussion and, more importantly, action through the adoption of best practices tailored to the unique circumstances of individual companies and their boards.

Chapter 20: Building Boards for Companies in Bankruptcy

In a bankruptcy board search, of course, the mandate is to fill not just a single board seat but an entire board more or less from scratch, a condition that significantly complicates the task. In filling a single seat, determining the ideal characteristics of a new director is fairly straightforward, given that the qualities of all the other players are established. One knows the boardroom culture into which a new director must fit. In the post-Chapter 11 case in the US however, there is no pre-existing boardroom culture, only an empty table.

Solving any equation with 10 or 12 unknown variables is a daunting task. To make the situation even more challenging, there almost always is significant time pressure, given that a board slate must be submitted several weeks before the hearing date set by the judge overseeing the case, and the exercise of naming a board usually gets pushed to the end of the bankruptcy process due to all the critical and contentious issues that also must be resolved, such as negotiating with banks and unions, before the composition of the board even can be considered. Thus, putting together a board does not begin until time is short and nerves are frayed from the heated arguments that have occurred along the way.

From the perspective of the search firm advising the search committee, the charged nature of a restructured company board search usually is apparent from the beginning since the first task is to convince all parties represented on the committee; debtors, management and creditors (sometimes joined by incumbent directors) that the search firm will be an objective facilitator that cannot favour one side over another. Fortunately, this normally is fairly easy to accomplish, given that the search committee's suspicions generally have more to do with each other than with any third party. It also is part of the search consultant's initial role to educate the search committee on the charge and keep the committee focused on the problem at hand. Unlike a standard search committee, which usually is composed of board directors who often are current or former CEOs and, thus, are well-versed in boardroom matters, a restructured company search committee frequently is largely populated by creditor representatives with limited direct experience in corporate governance issues.

In an assignment to fill a single director seat, the first step is to develop a list of attributes likely to be required in that person perhaps expertise in marketing or corporate finance, experience in emerging markets or track record as a change agent as well as to identify the desired management style and governance philosophy to complement or counterbalance the existing board's personalities. When the charge is to fill an entire board, however, one must construct a list to cover the competencies needed by the entire group, as well as the collective governance style best suited to the task of moving the company forward. Getting consensus on the list of attributes that becomes the filter against which potential candidates are screened usually is one of the least contentious steps in the process. The difficulty, however, comes later, in assembling the right combination of table pounders and conciliators up-through the ranks traditionalists and entrepreneurs, industry veterans and those from entirely different fields to result in a cohesive team that can provide a wide range of counsel and oversight to the new management.

Bankruptcy board searches are an illuminating case study in the dynamics of corporate governance.

The Search Begins

Ultimately, all parties agree on a wish list of candidates to approach. The executive search team further augments the list so that there are eight to 10 candidates for each seat to be filled. Doing so involves not only extensive database searching and research but also a great deal of internal discussion and discreet plying of sourcing networks to go past the usual suspects:

1. Who are the rising executives on the cusp of being elevated to CEO?
2. Which CEOs might be near retirement and thus able to take on a new challenge?
3. Who looks great on paper but might not have the temperament to shine in a turnaround scenario or who might be burdened with disqualifying conflicts?

Since some executives reject post-restructuring directorships out of hand, some potential candidates will be sounded out in general terms on the opportunity. (Such scepticism often is misplaced, given that companies emerging from bankruptcy are doing so with a clean slate. It is a pre-bankruptcy board one wants to avoid joining.) The process then returns to the search committee where the candidates are reviewed one by one. In addition to the pool that has been submitted, members of the search committee sometimes will have suggestions of their own. There is nothing wrong with that as long as these candidates undergo the same process of scrutiny and analysis as everyone else. The premise of emerging from bankruptcy is a clean slate so no one candidate should have an inside track to an oversight role.

The New Board Takes Shape

As the shaping of the board begins, the perspectives of the various players on the search committee become readily apparent. While debtors, management and creditors all have the same ultimate goal for the company in question to successfully emerge from bankruptcy they each are likely to have different priorities in how that is accomplished. For example, the debtors, who likely will be holding stock in the reorganized entity, might favour high-profile directors who will catch the eye of the business press and analysts and who will inspire confidence among shareholders.

The new management, however, might have little interest in that brand of sex appeal, focusing instead on executives with purely functional expertise who can be counted upon to roll up their sleeves and be an active resource. And the creditors whose ties with the company generally end on or shortly after emergence usually are looking for all tasks to be wrapped up on schedule with a minimum of disruption. Board composition like everything else in the bankruptcy process, even down to the location of meetings is viewed by the participants as a zero-sum negotiation.

The key to success is for members of the search committee to recognize that a range of abilities and approaches on the board will ensure that multiple objectives can be met, and this balanced composition makes for a strong board. Accomplishing this, however, demands a candidate pool that is both deep and wide enough to provide an array of options for each constituency. It also places a premium on identifying and highlighting candidates whose attributes satisfy multiple criteria for example, a CEO who has overseen the shift from commodity to multiple product lines or a marketing chief who has significant international experience. So it is that 10 names per seat usually are winnowed to six, which is further cut to four once another round of due diligence uncovers disqualifying conflicts that were not readily apparent such as a relative who is an executive at a supplier.

With the candidate pool now at 30 to 40 people, the search committee schedules several separate, full-day interview sessions. Interviewing candidates in a compressed time frame gives the search committee the additional benefit of comparing and contrasting candidates with each other and gaining a vivid sense of the chemistry mix offered by various candidate combinations. Interviews typically last an hour and centre on the aspects of the candidate's career most relevant to the challenges faced by the emerging company; prior board experience; views on management/ board relations, roles and responsibilities; and ability to commit the necessary time and energy.

During the third interview day, incumbent directors who wish to be considered for the new board are interviewed along with the remaining candidates. This sets up the interesting dynamic of directors being interviewed not only by their peers (the other incumbent directors, if any, on the search committee) but by the debtors and creditors with whom they have been in heated and frequently acrimonious negotiations for the past several months. Not surprisingly, there often is an extra layer of cordiality as everyone tries to set aside past conflicts at least for the moment. But no matter how well-behaved everyone is, it is an uphill battle for an incumbent to stay on the reorganized board.

The premise of emerging from bankruptcy is a clean slate so no one candidate should have an inside track to an oversight role. The first thing candidates usually want to know is who will be in the foxhole with them.

Solving the Equation

After time for reflection, the search committee convenes again to make its selections. At this critical, high-pressure stage, some committees may revert to a zero-sum perspective and treat the proceedings like a major league sports draft, complete with I'll-give-you-yours-if-you-give-me-mine horse trading. Instead, committee members need to look at the big picture. After all, it is not a question of trading one candidate for another but rather solving an equation with 12 variables. And in focusing on how various combinations of people are likely to interact, there will be numerous occasions in which an excellent candidate will have to be cut from the list because he or she would unbalance, in one way or another, the board being built. Those hard decisions will have to be made collectively in the common ground that has been identified between each group's line in the sand of non-negotiable.

Finally, somehow, the dust settles, and a consensus is reached. Offers are extended and inevitable questions must be addressed. The first thing candidates usually want to know is who else has been asked to serve who, in other words, will be in the foxhole with them? Prospective directors also will want a sense that the company really is working with a clean slate, with a new management team and a minimum of incumbent directors. Many times, evaluating the suitability of the incumbent CEO and senior management team is first on the new board's agenda. Members will want to know if any major acquisitions or divestitures are expected during the first year, given the significant due diligence work involved in

160

those transactions, as well as upon which committees they might be asked to serve. For instance, offers that include requests to serve on the audit committee frequently bring serious pushback.

There also will be standard inquiries about time commitments and logistics, including the frequency of board meetings outside the country and the possibility of phone participation. This last detail carries real significance: No one wants to be the person who dutifully treks across the country to a board meeting only to find that half the colleagues are phoning in. Given the challenges and time commitment of being a director of a company emerging from bankruptcy, why would someone accept in the first place? Just as some executives are drawn to start-ups or international postings, some simply are attracted to being part of a turnaround an exciting fresh start for an enterprise. Others might have a particular fascination with the industry in question or see the experience as an important professional development opportunity. (If they are not retired, they likely will have to convince their own company's governance committee that there is a good reason to serve on this board before formally accepting.)

Once the board is in place, the search committee usually convenes in a one- to two-day orientation session in which the incoming directors are briefed by the company's new management and key creditors, and time is scheduled so the directors have the chance to get to know each other and agree on how they will work together (including settling upon a work plan). This provides an opportunity for the board members to begin to outline their mandate prior to the formal assumption of fiduciary responsibility on the day the company emerges from bankruptcy.

The difficulty is in assembling the right combination of table pounders and conciliators, up-through-the-ranks traditionalists and entrepreneurs, industry veterans and those from entirely different fields.

Lessons to Consider

Building a board for a company emerging from bankruptcy is a special case in many ways. At the same time, however, there are several lessons that apply to more conventional director searches.

Look for candidates who can satisfy multiple skill sets. It is inevitable that several members of the search committee will have strong ideas about the qualities that a new director should possess. It is worth the investment of energy to try and find those candidates who can meet multiple criteria.

Think through a new director's impact on the culture of the board. Adding a new director is not just compiling a list of competencies. He or she and the respective unique leadership style will affect the dynamics of the board. The implications of choosing a particular candidate need to be weighed in the decision-making process.

Follow a structured process. Given that the search committee likely has a great deal of experience working together, it can be tempting to cut corners in certain aspects of the selection process. But being deliberate about each step determining criteria and sourcing and evaluating candidates not only leads to better results but to a clearer understanding of the board's strengths and weaknesses, culture and the particular way in which it exercises its oversight role.

Chapter 21: CEO Guide to Innovation

Organizations today are under more pressure than ever before to Innovate to actively strive for new ideas, continuous improvement, or where necessary, market disruption and to achieve these goals with both speed and purpose. But it's not just the "leading-edge" companies that are making innovation a priority.

Driving innovation is imperative for any organization operating in today's environment of relentless competition and unprecedented complexity. The CEO we interview around the world cited that innovation was the world number one challenge facing their organizations.

In fact, many organizations are acting on this need to innovate. In recent years, companies such as DuPont, Coca-Cola, Citigroup, SAP, and Owens Corning have appointed chief innovation officers whose full-time roles involve leading and bringing structure to innovation efforts and some have taken additional steps. For example, the French wine and spirits producer Pernod Ricard has established a Breakthrough Innovation Group and hired "innovation specialists" charged with facilitating idea generation.

What is your organization's unique innovation imperative? Do you need to enter new markets, grow sales, or expand your margins?

Do you need to become faster, better, more nimble, and adaptable? Do you need to deliver a killer combination of speed, quality, and low prices? (It used to be that an organization was only expected to deliver on two of those three. That has changed.)

Do you need to contain costs or streamline processes? Perhaps you need to do all of these?

Innovation is defined in many different ways. For instance, it is often thought of as a strategy or a system of processes and tools.

However, we see innovation as something more:
An act of leadership

Leaders are the embodiment of their organization and its way of believing, thinking, and doing. As CEO, the quality of your leadership will determine whether innovation succeeds or fails. You provide the values, vision, direction, and passion, which are far more important to success than a set of innovation tools or processes.

Innovation vs. Invention vs. Creativity

The terms "innovation," "invention," and "creativity" are often used interchangeably. Yet, they aren't synonymous, and the distinctions between them are important to keep in mind as you work to make innovation flourish in your organization. Innovation is the process of bringing new solutions to market that drive differentiation and measurable business value. Business strategies, processes, and solutions that are applied internally can also be targets for innovation. Innovation is not a solo act. It's a unique social phenomenon that requires the contributions of multiple collaborators who play critical roles to get things done.

Invention is creating something new that may or may not have a measurable business value. It is typically the out-come of research and experimentation. Unlike innovation, invention can reflect the work of a single individual.

Creativity is best viewed as an individual personality attribute. An individual may be creative in that he or she is able to generate many unique ideas (or build on others' ideas in value-added ways). Creativity fuels invention. But an individual who is creative may lack the skills, discipline, and ability needed to bring an idea to fruition and grow it into a meaningful innovation.

Innovation can assume multiple forms and help to achieve multiple objectives making it both fascinating and necessary. Innovation runs the spectrum from incremental to disruptive, and it can impact both the "What's" (products, services) and the "How's" (strategies, processes, systems, etc.).

Disruptive innovations change the game, and often create obsolescence (think of the fate of VHS video tapes once DVDs appeared). Incremental innovations, meanwhile, typically centre on making improvements that result in new solutions with value to the marketplace (such as the new features included in the release of a new version of software, such as Microsoft Office). That's not to say, however, that all disruptive innovation must happen on a large scale or that incremental innovations can't have a sizable impact. Nor are theses extremes the only two possible degrees of innovation. Innovations to individual components or to a process architecture can represent a middle ground.

As a CEO concerned with making innovation of all stripes part of your organization's brand, your focus needs to be on creating the conditions for repeatable innovation conditions that make both disruptive and incremental innovations possible. You need to understand these conditions and drive their absorption throughout the entire organization.

It's not about driving an initiative, however. While the work of innovation is often carried out by executing a number of initiatives, innovation itself shouldn't be thought of and approached as an initiative any more than, say, cost containment, talent management, or execution. Instead, innovation must become an organizational persona, demonstrated day in and day out via the behaviour of both leaders and employees. This requires organizational commitment, discipline, systems, and ongoing, everyday action. It also requires adopting new mindsets, behaviours, and norms. Above all else, innovation is enabled or constrained by your organization's culture. Culture is often defined in terms of the norms, values, and expectations that drive people. It has perhaps best been defined as "the way things get done around here," a pithy, yet altogether true description. Culture also can be thought of as your organization's "operational brand."

If you don't have a culture that can promote, support, and sustain Innovation; if innovation isn't an ingrained part of "the way things get done around here" you won't be able to create and sustain the conditions required for innovation. Also, the organization's readiness and ability to embrace the risks and rewards of innovation will be limited, if not non-existent. As CEO, it is up to you to take deliberate and sustained action to make innovation part of your organization's culture i.e., its organizational persona and its operational brand as well as part of your own leadership brand, which, in turn, will define your leadership legacy.

But, of course, it's not easy. Consider the challenges that arise when an organization's intent to innovate is offset by deeply entrenched cultural mores that may run counter to, and may seriously impede, its aspirations to innovate.

An organization that has grown steadily and profitably through acquisition has turned to innovation as an organic growth strategy.

An organization that has a long history of doing everything "in house" has determined it is time to outsource product development to more quickly get products to market.

An organization for which technology has never been a core competency wants to keep pace with, and move ahead of, upstart competitors by offering technology cantered products.

A traditionally risk-averse senior team with little change management experience seeks to grow by entering new global markets characterized by more aggressive competitors than the organization has encountered in its core markets. As these challenges illustrate, innovation can and should test the organization's self-perceived assumptions, its aspirations and, by extension, its identity. In its most disruptive form, innovation can lead an organization out of its comfort zone and away from markets and businesses where it has had success in the past.

Consider Apple's move into the music and cellular phone businesses, General Motors rolling out the Chevy Volt hybrid car, and Taiwan Mobile's transition from a traditional telecomm company to a "digital convergence" company based on the integration of mobile phones, computers, and

TVs all innovations that moved these organizations away from their core businesses ones that required strong and committed leadership at the top. Indeed, the purposeful shifts away from the tried, true, and profitable that sometimes accompany innovation can challenge CEO, and his or her vision and leadership in real and meaningful ways.

Being a CEO is a frenetic exercise in juggling priorities, but it's an exercise guided by one objective: balancing the demands of the present with the needs of the future. CEO's must focus on meeting short-term sales and financial goals, outmanoeuvring the competition, keeping product rollouts on target, managing costs, and navigating the regulatory environment, while at the same time shaping and reinforcing the organization's future by formulating a vision, anticipating the emergence of future markets, setting long-term strategy, and growing the talent the organization needs for tomorrow.

Innovation falls into the latter category. It's a future-focused strategy that exists on an even plane of importance with other critical demands. In fact, the raft of conflicting priorities and the perpetual impatience of investors and other key stakeholders seem to get in the way of innovation.

What also makes innovation especially challenging is that the decisions made and the actions taken to instil and sustain innovation can have a large-scale impact on the organization.

As CEO, you need to focus on both long-term and short-term priorities, keeping the company profitable now while driving the right innovation strategy needed for the future. We refer to this complex reality as the Innovation Paradox. Charles Holliday, Jr., the former CEO of DuPont, accurately captured one of the most vexing aspects of the Innovation

Paradox when he said that "the stock market pays you for what you can do now," and that it's tough to get investors to think more than two years ahead."

In addition to the struggle between the short and long term, the Innovation Paradox encompasses struggles that a CEO must grapple with:

- How to mobilize the company and its people to embrace the new and different.
- How to build a pipeline of new ideas, and ensure that the most promising ones are explored.
- How to invest adequate manpower and resources in "non-core" projects while still getting the everyday work done.
- How to promote innovation without putting the company's financial viability and competitive position at risk.
- How to balance the need to give people freedom to innovate while maintaining organizational control.
- How to bring process and discipline to innovation.

The full impact of the Innovation Paradox comes into sharper focus when you consider the many things you must actually do to drive innovation, many of which appear to be counterintuitive, or otherwise fly in the face of your typical leadership style. Among them:

- You don't need to be the one who comes up with breakthrough ideas (though you should freely contribute your own ideas). You need to create an environment in which others can generate ideas, while you retain accountability for the ultimate outputs.
- You don't and can't make every decision tied to execution. You need to empower others to make

169

decisions and then be willing to explain and defend those decisions.

- You need to drive accountability while disseminating responsibility down through the ranks, yet be willing to take action, when needed.
- You need to provide the time, freedom, and resources required to achieve ambitious innovation goals, while keeping execution moving at breakneck speed.
- You need to model open-mindedness and value different opinions, perspectives, and approaches, while promoting consistency and reinforcing the organization's strategic direction.

Above all, as CEO you must be a champion for taking appropriate risks and supporting experimentation. However, the "new and different" outcomes associated with innovation are never a sure thing. The gains promised by innovation rarely happen without iteration and openness to occasional misfires or even "failure." As the list above suggests, innovation requires a wholly unique leadership approach. The way in which you have led your organization may not prove helpful in driving innovation; you need to view innovation differently.

Through research we conducted, we sought to understand what is required for innovation to establish roots, become repeatable and sustainable, and drive differentiation. The result of our research is a model that identifies four inherent innovation challenges ones that probably keep you up at night:

- Failure to understand stakeholders (i.e., both internal and external, such as clients, partners, consumers, senior leaders, and other departments).

- Lacklustre ideas (i.e., old ways of thinking, narrow ideas, ideas that don't pinpoint the heart of the problem).
- Aversion to risk taking (i.e., failure to push new boundaries, playing it safe, conflict avoidance).
- Poor execution (i.e., creative ideas simply remain ideas).

Keep in mind that the four points above are not level-specific; all leaders, from CEO down to frontline supervisors, must take accountability for them:

- To overcome failure to understand stakeholders, leaders must Inspire Curiosity in their employees by showing them how to adopt a stance of humility and providing intellectual stimulation to learn about the people for whom they are providing solutions. To help do this, leaders themselves need to exhibit curiosity about a wide range of topics including those topics that are unrelated to the business.

- To overcome lacklustre ideas, leaders must Challenge Current Perspectives by pushing boundaries, creating and sharing compelling aspirations, and providing ideation methods that provoke thinking. Leaders need to be adept at helping others think beyond the confines of the way things are usually conceived of and executed. They must inspire others to think in terms of "What if?" instead of "What?".

- To overcome aversion to risk taking, leaders must Provide Freedom to empower their people to take risks on new and different ideas. When leaders take the risk out of risk-taking, they allow for potentially game changing ideas and solutions. Senior leaders, especially CEO, need to be willing to commit organizational resources, including time, money, and talent, to promote innovation and advance the exploration of new ideas and execution of new solutions.

- To overcome poor execution, leaders must Drive Discipline by providing focus, accountability, engagement, and sustainability to the execution process. They also need to devote the same structure and focus to innovation as to other critical organizational priorities.

Chapter 22: CEO Guide to Leadership Development

"The difference between involvement and commitment is like ham and eggs. The chicken is involved; the pig is committed. The biggest differentiator of companies that excel in leadership development is the commitment and ownership of CEO or top executive". – Ade Asefeso

Don't you hate it when people quote themselves?

It's easy for a "chicken" CEO to just pay lip service to leadership development. All they need to do is show up at the annual talent review and nod their heads; stop by a few training programs to give a quick talk, approve the training budget, and read the script written for them by HR that tells them to say, "People are our most important assets" at every employee gathering.

You can tell what is really important to them by taking a look at their calendar to see where they spend their time, the agenda items on their executive team meetings, and by what gets measured.

So when it comes to leadership development, what is the difference between a CEO that is just "involved" and one that is really committed?

Here are 10 things that I believe would give any CEO the best return on their time invested. The good news is that none of these involve spending much money, and they may already be doing many of them:

1. Focus on results and don't let the process be the tail wagging the dog.

I've seen way too many organizations get caught up in the process and lose sight of the results. They create complicated processes and forms, thick binders, have long meetings, and put way too much importance on impressing their board of directors in their annual talent review. Once the meeting is over, the binder gets set aside and nothing happens until the next year. VPs and senior managers soon catch on that it's nothing but an exercise and focus on looking good instead of being good.

This doesn't mean the annual CEO and board reviews are not important; it's been my experience that if you don't do this, then nothing happens. Events, like annual check-ups, force things to happen that otherwise get pushed aside because they are not urgent.

2. Have high expectations for the head of HR.

CEO's HR partner not only needs to know all of the best practices and processes, but they have to have the ability to influence and be trusted by the executive team as well as be CEO's trusted adviser on talent. It's a tough balance; they may be coaching a struggling VP one day and recommending to CEO the same VP be replaced the next day. They have to be able to play match-maker and broker job changes, and manage all of the ego and politics involved.

3. Practice what you preach.

Committed CEOs publicly work on their own leadership development, then work on the development of their executive team. They coach them, give them feedback, and develop individual development plans with them. They support their development. A CEO's behaviours are powerful; they set the expectations for the rest of the management team, creating a trickle-down effect of leadership development.

4. Know how executives really develop.

Think back on your career where and how did you learn your most valuable leadership lessons? It was probably:

- New jobs
- Challenging assignments
- From other people (good and bad bosses, a coach, mentors, etc.)
- Courses, books, articles, and other means

Too many companies spend too much time on the last bullet point; it's not only the least effective, it's lazy. The top companies understand it's all about learning through experience. When you think about it, it's a sunk cost you might as well leverage it. Don't get me wrong courses can be effective, when they are designed in ways that incorporate the other points.

5. Be the CTB (Chief Talent Broker)

While there are challenges to cross-functional movement of high potentials, somehow the companies best at leadership development figure out how to do it without damaging the business and ruining careers. They intentionally move their HIPOs high potentials from job to job to get them ready for bigger jobs.

If it's left up to each manager, it won't happen. Why should they? It's certainly not in their best interests to give up their best talent. CEO is the only one (other than the HR Vice President) looking at leadership development from a what is best for the company, long-range perspective. Managers won't do it or even see value in it unless CEO establishes it as an expectation and encourages them to give up their top talent and be willing to accept (and develop) unlikely developmental candidates.

6. Spend time assessing talent.

Assessing talent is all about having regular talent reviews, conducting formal assessments, and spending time with high-potentials. Know what to look for, too indicators of success in larger roles isn't the same as performance in a current role. Astute CEOs know how to ask the questions, what behaviours to look for, and the difference between performance (results) and leadership potential.

7. Hold others accountable for assessing and developing future leaders.

All too often companies will conduct talent reviews and succession plan reviews and discuss development then, a year later, nothing happens. A CEO needs to establish the vision, set meaningful goals, measure them, and hold people accountable. It takes time to change a culture, but a few public coronations and hangings help send the message that it's important.

8. Stay involved in company leadership development programs.

Yes, CEOs should keep sponsoring those executive development programs and show up to speak; that is a good start. However, committed CEOs don't just show up at the beginning and end they teach in programs, get to know participants and help set program objectives and measures.

9. Keep the board engaged

CEO's board is involved in all of the other strategic aspects of the business why not leadership development? Board members can be valuable sources of insight, advice and connections, and their support is important when it's time to make key talent decisions.

10. Take decisive action on underperformers

Entrenched underperformers block the development and advancement of an organization's high potentials. When I've conducted 9 box meetings, leadership teams often clam up when I try to engage them in this discussion. They don't do a good job differentiating (everybody's a B or A, and nobody's a C), and they are too hesitant or slow to take action. I think, in general, most companies are too tolerant and slow to act.

Chapter 23: CEO Guide to Preparing Future Global Leaders

Globalization means a blossoming of business opportunities as never before. New markets are available to firms with the resources to get their goods and services in front of customers; purveyors of Starbucks, McDonald's, Ferrari, and Gucci not only line the streets of London or Chicago, but Melbourne and Shanghai as well.

In many ways, customers, suppliers, and capital are the easiest pieces of the global puzzle to assemble, especially when compared to developing a leadership team to manage that puzzle profitably. The companies that invest in developing global leadership talent find new opportunities and better execution, while companies that don't face new risks and potential failure of their multinational strategy.

Although most organizations today understand the need to be global, many still focus solely on building the infrastructure for global expansion (logistics, information technology, financial systems) and do not invest enough time and effort into identifying, selecting and developing the talent necessary to succeed globally. Leadership on the global stage is different and smart companies are increasing their investment in developing global leaders who can deliver results in far-flung markets around the world.

Are You Building a Global Leadership Talent Pool?

If your organization is unsatisfied or unsure of the quality of its global leadership base, the following questions may help you to develop your global leadership talent pool:

1. Willingness: Does your organization recognize the need to build a global leadership talent pool? Are you and other leaders ready to move in that direction?
2. Resources: Are you willing and able to put the time, effort, money, and intangible resources against global leadership identification, selection, and development?
3. Talent: Do you have the potential talent on board to jumpstart your global leadership initiative or will you have to look beyond your organization's walls?
4. Human resources skills: Do you possess the HR talent and tools and/or the consulting expertise at your side to make global leadership a reality in your organization?

If you answered yes to all of the above, then your organization is ready to start down a path to global leadership that will enable it to leverage new markets, attract new customers, find new sources of capital and grow beyond your wildest expectations.

Chapter 24: CEO Guide to Crisis Management

This chapter is about the interview we had with a FTSE 100 CEO in London UK.

Interviewer: With the economy tanking, what leadership skills are most in demand now? Joining me today to talk about this is a CEO of FTSE 100 company.

CEO: Well it's an interesting time. Glad to be here.

Interviewer: Certainly is. We have got so many businesses in turmoil, what are the leadership skills and experiences that are really at a premium now?

CEO: From a board's perspective: communication skills, agility and decisiveness.

Interviewer: And why is that?

CEO: I think different times call for different leadership traits. Some people can adapt to them; some people have to bring those traits with them. Agility, that it's all moving so fast; a business plan from six months ago even six days ago doesn't matter anymore, literally, as we are seeing right now. Communication skills aren't only about the analysts and the shareholders, but internally. Are we going to survive? Where are we going? Can we take advantage of this, or are we going to suffer from this? It's all about those communication skills.

Interviewer: Yeah, I mean companies are really having to just rip up their game plans now.

CEO: Right, the agility is to say, I think, when you see the smartest companies are saying, "Ok we are at an incredible crisis, what can we do to take advantage of it? Is there a product or a service or a marketing story that positions us differently now." Whereas other companies are saying, "Woe is me, this is terrible." I think the most agile leaders are saying we are going to move as fast as we can to take advantage of a crisis.

Interviewer: And now how is that different from the leadership skills and experiences that are in demand in calmer economic times?

CEO: You see things in cycles. If you look at the internet era, it was the vision thing. In the last economic downturn, it was about operational profitability, and then it was about global – China, India, offshore, outsourcing. And now you see people who have to react. You see people who must be very quick in decision-making even in capital intensive manufacturing businesses, which tend to have much longer product times. General Motors is reacting by the hour.

Interviewer: So the skills for this crisis are actually even different from the skills in the last downturn?

CEO: There is no question. In the last downturn, people had more time to react, and they probably had greater certainty about liquidity, greater certainty about the strength of their partners and vendors, and now you don't have certainty about who is strong and who's not strong.

Interviewer: I want to ask you about boards as well; we saw a number of very high profile boards that were caught off guard, and sort of ill-prepared for the crisis. How does that change what you are looking for in a director and the advice that you give boards?

CEO: You tended to have people who understood the industry, and circles close to it. Now we are saying, "I need someone who understands risk management. I need someone who understands capital markets. I need someone who understands messaging." And so it's very functional as well as reacting to the markets' immediacy.

Interviewer: Thanks so much for joining me.

CEO: It's an interesting time. Thanks for asking.

Chapter 25: CEO Guide to Succession Planning

The transition from one CEO to another is a critical moment in a company's history. A smooth transition is essential to maintain the confidence of investors, business partners, customer and employees, and provides the incoming CEO with a solid platform from which to move the company forward. A properly designed and executed succession plan is at the centre of any successful transition.

CEO vacancies can be planned or unplanned; in either scenario, by the time a succession plan is needed it is far too late to start building one. Because of this, it is the responsibility of the board to make succession planning a priority, even in the face of more immediate and tangible issues. In addition to being necessary for risk mitigation, succession planning brings with it several beneficial by-products.

- It provides a framework that drives senior executive development, aligning leadership at the top of the enterprise with the strategic needs of the firm.
- It gives CEO, through an ongoing analysis of the job requirements, the opportunity to adjust his or her role in light of changing business conditions and strategic imperatives.
- It strengthens the relationship and information flow between the board and the senior management team through the regular contact that is part of the board's review of candidates.

AA Global Sourcing Ltd regularly advises boards and CEOs on Chief Executive Officer Succession Planning, and from this experience we have developed the following practical guide to the succession planning process.

## 1.	Establishing the Foundation

Succession planning is usually directed by the governance or compensation committees, or occasionally a special ad hoc committee. The current CEO's involvement varies (depending on whether the succession is planned or unexpected) with primary responsibility being the development of internal candidates. The Lead Director often acts as the single point of contact between the board and the sitting CEO on succession matters.

Create a written succession plan

This document should detail how the company's officers are elected and replaced, how successors are to be chosen and the respective roles of CEO, the board and the various board committees in the succession process. Emergency succession procedures, in the case of sudden death or vacancy, are also included. Agreeing on these elements before there is a need to implement them helps ensure an orderly, deliberate transition while avoiding uncertainty and destabilizing political manoeuvring.

Conduct regular, in-depth reviews

The entire board, together with a senior human resources executive, should review the succession plan twice a year, including an examination of the relevant bylaws and succession procedures and a review of the baseline capabilities requirements for the next CEO a working document that summarizes what these requirements would be if the search for a new CEO were held today.

To determine those requirements, the board should begin by examining company direction and strategy over a five to fifteen year time period, factoring in the impact of various scenarios such as how the business will be affected by challenges including the continuing globalization of supply chains, customers, competitors and investors, or the risks and opportunities brought by changing climate and global health conditions. Looking at the impact of broad trends such as these helps ensure that the company's next leader will have the capabilities and experience necessary to respond to unfolding complex events across numerous fronts. The board should also use this opportunity to observe successful CEOs from both inside and outside the industry and identify traits that have contributed to particular success.

The board then distils these considerations into a set of required capabilities. AA Global Sourcing Ltd Assessment Framework offers one model to work from. Based on the company's situation and strategic direction; some capabilities will be deemed essential and others of secondary or little importance.

Compare the resulting list of capabilities against the firm's senior talent pipeline.

While human resources manages the day-to-day aspects of measuring development, the board should be briefed annually and have regular exposure to internal candidates through board presentations, field observations and site visits. Revise the leadership development plan of each candidate as needed to address progress and shortcomings.

Boards can decide to bolster this talent pipeline by recruiting from outside. This requires significant advance planning; bringing in a senior executive who could potentially go on to fill CEO role typically requires a three-year lead time so that the candidate will have fully been absorbed into the firm's culture by the time that the elevation takes place.

Narrow the field to two or three finalists.

This typically occurs two years from the planned date of CEO transition, with input from the full board and CEO. The final round of professional development for the candidates should be designed so that they are exposed to multiple aspects of the business and are given responsibility for key initiatives such as overseeing entry into a new geographic region or the integration of an acquisition that will mirror the sorts of complex challenges they would have as CEO while giving the board an opportunity to evaluate their performance.

Although there will be plenty of internal and external speculation at this point in the succession process, it is important to defuse any aura of competition that may develop; finalists should not be pitted against each other, but given separate domains in which to lead and the opportunity to build programs that will contribute to the company's profitability over a sustained period.

2. Implementing the Plan

Assess the finalist candidates.

Approximately one year before the planned transition, the full board should meet to implement the succession plan. CEO competency list should be given a final review and revised as necessary. The board should then implement a thorough assessment of the finalist candidates, including:

- In-depth competency-focused interviews that probe for the skills and talents essential for the role.
- 360° referencing that provides added insight from superiors, industry peers, colleagues and direct reports.
- Online psychometric testing, interpreted by an in-house psychologist, which gives shape to intangible qualities.

Measure internal candidates against their peers at other firms.

This will ensure the company is choosing the best CEO available, rather than merely the best choice from within its own ranks. The customary approach is to turn to independent senior search consultants, who then identify the most appropriate candidates in the marketplace. This list often includes not only candidates from within the industry in question but those from adjacent industries as well, to ensure that all of the best candidates are being considered.

On the basis of this information and the many other data points which have been amassed during the assessment period, internal candidates and the external benchmark candidates are given numerical rankings across the various required competencies. The board's governance committee, usually with the assistance of outside consultants, also produces a detailed written evaluation.

Finally, the board deliberates and makes its final decision.

If the board cannot come to an agreement on an internal candidate, it will need to conduct an external search to widen the pool. However, the foundation for an external search, including identified CEO competencies and the list of external benchmark candidates, is already in place.

3.   The Successful Transition

Once a final candidate has been selected, it is critical that a thorough transition plan be developed so that the new CEO has the benefit of a strong start. A solid transition spans a full year, and contains five phases:

a.   Begin intensive knowledge sharing.

The outgoing and incoming CEO meet frequently for in-depth discussion regarding the operating styles, histories and expectations of board members and senior management, as well as other stakeholder constituencies, including investors, creditors, customers, analysts and regulators. At various points, individual members of the senior management team are included in the discussion. Third-party interviews can help prevent the biasing of information.

b.   Communicate with stakeholders.

Following this briefing period, the incoming CEO should be introduced to the company's stakeholders in a series of information-gathering sessions. This allows the outgoing CEO to gracefully pass the baton and for the incoming CEO to build support and good will with various key players, especially those he or she has not dealt with before.

c. Develop a written transition plan.

With the involvement and support of the senior management team, a detailed timeline is then developed to provide the orderly transition of roles and responsibilities. If the appointment is an internal promotion, this includes the elevation of the executive who takes over the new CEO's former position. If the outgoing CEO is remained as Chairman, that role needs to be clearly defined so as to not interfere with the new CEO.

d. Share the transition plan.

The plan needs to be effectively communicated internally and externally to project a sense of stability and positive perspective. Appropriate recognition of the outgoing CEO is an important component; failing to show appreciation for an outgoing leader's legitimate accomplishments risks alienating his or her supporters in the company and on the board.

e. Strengthen relationships with the board.

Even if the new CEO is known to the board, it is important that they begin to relate to him or her in the new role through one-on-one meetings. If the new CEO is appointed from within, he or she can begin to be phased into board meetings over a period of time. To the extent possible, the outgoing CEO should provide coaching and feedback to his or her successor throughout the process.

Chapter 26: CEO Guide to CEO's Compensation

It's hard to read the business news without coming across reports about the salaries, bonuses, and stock option packages awarded to chief executives of publicly traded companies. Making sense of the numbers to assess how companies are paying their top brass isn't always easy. Is executive compensation working in the favour of investors? Here are a few guidelines for checking a company's compensation program.

Risk and Reward

Company boards, at least in principle, try to use compensation contracts to align executives' actions with company success. The idea is that CEO performance provides value to the organization. "Pay for performance" is the mantra most companies use when they try to explain their compensation plans.

While everyone can support the idea of paying for performance, it implies that CEOs take on risk. CEOs' fortunes should rise and fall with companies' fortunes. When you are looking at a company's compensation program, it's worth checking to see how much stake executives have in delivering the goods for investors. Let's take a look at how different forms of compensation put a CEO's reward at risk if performance is poor.

Cash/Base Salaries

These days, it's common for CEOs to receive base salaries well over $1 million. In other words, CEO gets a terrific reward when the company does well, but still receives the reward when the company does badly. On their own, big base salaries offer little incentive for executives to work harder and make smart decisions.

Bonuses

Be careful about bonuses. In many cases, an annual bonus is nothing more than a base salary in disguise. A CEO with a $1 million salary may also receive a $700,000 bonus. If any of that bonus, say $500,000, does not vary with performance, then CEO's real salary is $1.5 million.

Watch: Fat Cats

Bonuses that vary with performance are another matter. It's hard to argue with the idea that CEOs who know they will be rewarded for performance tend to perform at a higher level. CEOs have an incentive to work hard.

Performance can be gauged by any number of things, such as profits or revenue growth, return on equity, or share price appreciation. But using simple measures to determine appropriate pay for performance can be tricky. Financial metrics and annual share price gains are not always a fair measure of how well an executive is doing his or her job. Executives can get unfairly penalized for one-time events and tough choices that might hurt performance or cause negative reactions from the market. It's up to the board of directors to create a balanced set of measures for judging CEO's effectiveness.

Stock Options

Companies trumpet stock options as the way to link executives' financial interests with shareholders' interests.

But options are far from perfect. In fact, with options, risk can get badly skewed. When shares go up in value, executives can make a fortune from options; but when they fall, investors lose out while executives are no worse off than before. Indeed, some companies let executives swap old option shares for new, lower-priced shares when the company's shares fall in value.

Worse still, the incentive to keep the share price motoring upward so that options will stay in-the-money encourages executives to focus exclusively on the next quarter and ignore shareholders' longer term interests. Options can even prompt top managers to manipulate the numbers to make sure the short-term targets are met. That hardly reinforces the link between CEOs and shareholders.

Stock Ownership

Academic studies say that common stock ownership is the most important performance driver. So, one way for CEOs to truly have their interests tied with shareholders is for them to own shares, not options. Ideally, that involves giving executives bonuses on the condition they use the money to buy shares. Face it; top executives act more like owners when they have a stake in the business.

Finding the Numbers

You can find a whole host of information on a company's compensation program in its regulatory filing. Form DEF 14A, filed with the Securities and Exchange Commission in the US, provides summary tables of compensation for a company's CEO and other highest paid executives.

When evaluating the base salary and annual bonus, investors like to see companies award a bigger chunk of compensation as bonus rather than base salary. The DEF 14A should offer an explanation of how the bonus is determined and what form the reward takes, whether cash, options, or shares.

Information on CEO stock option holdings can also be found in the summary tables. The form discloses the frequency of stock option grants and the amount of awards received by executives in the year. It also discloses re-pricing of stock options.

The proxy statement is where you can locate numbers on executives' "beneficial ownership" in the company. But do not ignore the table's accompanying footnotes. There you will find out how many of those shares the executive actually owns and how many are unexercised options. Again, it's reassuring to find executives with plenty of stock ownership.

Assessing CEO compensation is a bit of a black art. Interpreting the numbers isn't terribly straightforward. All the same, it's valuable for investors to get a sense of how compensation programs can create incentives or disincentives for top managers to work in the interests of shareholders.

Chapter 27: Motivational Quotes for CEOs

"Leadership is about empathy. It is about having the ability to relate and to connect with people for the purpose of inspiring and empowering their lives."
Oprah Winfrey

"My philosophy of leadership is to surround myself with good people who have ability, judgment and knowledge, but above all, a passion for service."
Sonny Perdue

"Some people have ideas. A few carry them into the world and make them happen. These are the innovators."
Andrew Mercer

"We tell our young managers, don't be afraid to make a mistake. But please don't make the same mistake twice."
Akio Morita

"When all is said and done, a lot more is said than done."
Lou Holtz

"Within an organization, a few qualities must be homogenous held in common by all. These are values, vision, and commitment to the team. However, in most areas, hiring for diversity is the wisest course of action. The strongest environments are inhabited by leaders with varied expertise, experiences, backgrounds, and temperaments."
John Maxwell

"All my life, whenever it comes time to make a decision, I make it and forget about it."
Harry S. Truman

"Leaders are more powerful role models when they learn than when they teach."
Rosabeth Moss Kantor

"It is better to lead from behind and to put others in front, especially when you celebrate victory when nice things occur. You take the front line when there is danger. Then people will appreciate your leadership."
Nelson Mandela

"I've said it over and over; when you get that one guy, you can win. A lot of times, one person can have a tremendous effect on a team."
Mike Ilitch - Owner Detroit Tigers and Detroit Red Wings

"We need our veterans to set an example, like being the first ones there. A veteran is entitled to a bigger pay cheque, but not a special set of rules."
Jim Leyland - Manager - Detroit Tigers

"We have played hard as a team and found ways to win. We have done that a lot, and you are optimistic those things can continue."
Mike Babcock - Detroit Red Wings Head Coach

"Big thinking precedes great achievement."
Wilferd Peterson

"A great leader's courage to fulfil his vision comes from passion, not position."
John Maxwell

"A manager is an assistant to his men."
Thomas J. Watson

"If I pick up the phone, I accept the responsibility to ensure the caller is satisfied, no matter what the issue is."
Michael Ramundo

"When you ask creative people how they did something, they feel a little guilty because they didn't really do it, they just saw something."
Steve Jobs

"I never perfected an invention that I did not think about in terms of the service it might give others... I find out what the world needs, then I proceed to invent."
Thomas Edison

"Capital isn't so important in business. Experience isn't so important. You can get both these things. What is important is ideas. If you have ideas, you have the main asset you need, and there isn't any limit to what you can do with your business and your life."
Harvey Firestone

"It is not the employer who pays the wages. Employers only handle the money. It is the customer who pays the wages."
Henry Ford

"Customers don't expect you to be perfect. They do expect you to fix things when they go wrong."
Donald Porter

"With businesses, you go to the same places because you like the service, you like the people and they take care of you. They greet you with a smile. That is how people want to be treated, with respect. That is what I tell my employees... customer service is very important."
Magic Johnson

"To be a leader is difficult, but to be regarded as a good leader is more difficult."
Ade Asefeso

"Teamwork means more 'we' and less 'me'. TEAM stands for: Together - Everyone - Achieves - More. We must learn to work as a unit. Unity is Strength."
Ade Asefeso

"When you go up the organizational hierarchy, do not forget to always stay in touch with reality."
Ade Asefeso

Chapter 28: Conclusion

(Year 1)
It's all you. Find a business partner with a complementary skill set if needed. Make sure you have $20,000 saved up to get started.   Focus on product development and getting something to market that solves a customer need. Create something of value to others and sell, sell, sell! Get customer feedback and use it to make your product better.

(Year 2)
- Do all you can to enable the company to survive.
- Build an Advisory Board.
- Hire your first employees.
- You should be in charge of product or sales or both.
- Set up a basic low cost office space.
- Outsource your payroll.

(Year 3)
- Hire an outside bookkeeper/accountant to produce monthly financial statements by the 20th of the following month.
- Put real time visible dashboards in place.
- Everyone won't report to you anymore.
- Start putting managers in place.
- Figure out your unit economics and consider raising funding to invest in growth.
- Hold a weekly meeting with either the whole company or all the key operational individuals.

- Hire people more experienced than yourself for the role you are hiring for, even if you have to wait a bit longer to be able to afford them.
- Keep the organization focused on selling and growing.
- Put in place an employee handbook.
- Define your values.
- Define your mission and vision.
- Put in place a formal performance review process and ensure a manager conversation and performance review is completed at least every 12 months, including 360 reviews in which peers and staff review their managers.
- Set up an options plan.
- Install a CRM system.

(Year 4)
- Start a weekly meeting with your Senior Leadership Team, Leadership Team, and Managers.
- Start a weekly meeting with just your Senior Leadership Team.
- Hire a Controller or CFO, a Director of Human Resources, and an Administrative Assistant.
- Make sure your Controller/CFO begins providing monthly accurate financial statements to you by the 20th of the following month in GAAP format and Managerial format.
- Document your systems and processes in an employee handbook.
- Set KPIs and have your team report on them weekly.
- Put in place documented incentive compensation systems.

- Think about creating systems to ease internal employee communication, like internal wikis, company meetings, external events, and retreats.
- Start using a One Page Strategic Plan with a quarterly theme.
- Have formal annual planning meetings to set or communicate both strategy and budgets for the upcoming year.
- Start investing consciously in shaping your company culture.
- Start investing consciously in managerial and leadership development courses for your managers and future managers.
- Hire an Auditor to audit your annual financial statements.

(Years 5/6)
- Define your company's hedgehog concept (what you can be the best in the world at, what you're passionate about, what drives your economic engine?).
- Implement The Five Dysfunctions of a Team Material throughout the organization.
- Launch a formal corporate social responsibility program.
- Start thinking about what new markets your organization can go into the future and figure out what your next product cycle will be.
- Think about what the next big thing will be in your broad industry and position your company to be the leader in it.
- Start top-grading your people and letting go of the bottom 10-20% annually.

- Constantly ask yourself what will be driving revenue growth most in 24 months?
- Put in place a system that will enable you and your leaders to know everyone's name.
- Launch an HRIS to automate your human resources functions like talent recruitment, performance management, compensation, and employee training.
- Implement the Service Profit Chain from Peak.
- Switch to a Big 4 Auditor.
- Launch a Corporate Development Department.
- Hire an Investment Bank If Needed to Evaluate M&A opportunities.

(Year 7+)
- Consider scaling yourself by hiring COO or separating the organization into different units with GMs or Presidents.
- Your role is now divided into five parts, described below.
  o Set Strategy and Vision
  o Manage the Senior Team
  o Communicate with Stakeholders
  o Oversee Resource Allocation
  o Build the Culture

Lessons I Learned as CEO

Here are the most important lessons I've learned over the years from 2010-2013.

Ten Most Important Lessons Learned As CEO

1. Just get started, have a bias toward action, and don't get stuck in analysis paralysis.

2. Build a product that just works and is so easy to use it doesn't require customer service.

3. To grow your sales, it is critical to calculate the lifetime value of an average customer, calculate what you're currently paying to acquire an average customer (total monthly ad spend divided by customers acquired in that month), determine the maximum you are willing to pay to acquire an average customer, and scale your marketing scientifically by testing relentlessly and finding the channels in which you can acquire customers for less than your maximum acceptable customer acquisition cost and then growing spend within those channels.

4. Never raise more equity capital than 1x your current annualized revenue (monthly revenue x 12). If you raise too much money too soon you will give up too much ownership and control of your company and be tempted to spend the money in ways that aren't carefully controlled. Wait to raise a large round until you have proven mathematically that $X amount of additional spending with generate $Y amount of additional revenue. (Once you figure out #3 this is easy). If you do choose to raise money, raise it from investors you like and get along with well. You will have to hang out with these people for the next 3-7 years, so make sure you enjoy spending time with them.

5. After the first year or two, your success is determined by the people you hire, not by you. Stop trying to do everything yourself. Scale yourself by hiring people more experienced than you in their field as soon as you can afford to.

6. Every member of the team should have a significant portion of their compensation based on the company's success and their department's success, quantified and communicated clearly in advance.

7. Your job as CEO is not to micromanage/tell your team members what to do, but rather to hire experienced people who can do their jobs better than you could, collaboratively set numerical goals, and hold your direct reports accountable for their performance individually and as a team.

8. Once you get past the start-up phase when you are responsible for everything, the six parts of a CEO's role are
   a. Set strategy and vision
   b. Manage the senior team
   c. Communicate with stakeholders
   d. Be the Customer Advocate
   e. Oversee resource allocation and
   f. Build the Culture.

9. It is possible to become more socially and environmentally responsible and increase your financial returns at the same time.

10. If you create a great culture (a fun work environment filled with people who are high performers and who

care about their work and their impact on the world) you will be able to attract and retain better people who will be much more engaged and productive and create a much more financially successful company.

Good Luck!!